A Taste of Buddhist Practice
Approaching Its Meaning and Its Ways

Advice from Thaye Dorje, the 17th Gyalwa Karmapa

A Taste of Buddhist Practice
Approaching Its Meaning and Its Ways

Advice from Thaye Dorje, the 17th Gyalwa Karmapa

RABSEL
PUBLICATIONS

RABSEL PUBLICATIONS
16, rue de Babylone
76430 La Remuée, France
www.rabsel.com
contact@rabsel.com

© Rabsel Publications, La Remuée, France, 2020

ISBN 978-2-36017-027-2

Table of Contents

Introductory Remarks
from the Editor

This book came out of a series of oral teachings that Thaye Dorje, the 17th Gyalwa Karmapa, transmitted during his visit to Grenoble, France from August 10–12, 2017. The text is a slightly edited transcription of five sessions of teachings that he gave in front of an audience of over two thousand people.

This book is not an exhaustive presentation of the topic of Buddhist meditation practice. As Karmapa himself explains in the beginning of his teaching, the goal is to "find a way to summarize the essential points and at the same time make sure that everyone is able to bring something with him or herself once the event is complete."

In general—and in particular during these three days—when Karmapa shares the Buddha's methods, he translates them from a distant time and an Eastern cultural context to the 21st century in the West. In other words, he makes these methods accessible without affecting their integrity. Free from the traps of seduction and fascination, he transmits their essential flavor so that both a beginner and a seasoned practitioner can taste them and integrate them.

The conversational style of the teaching—with a simple yet precise vocabulary—has been intentionally preserved. The wealth of synonyms Karmapa uses encourages us not to fixate on an understanding based on one particular term. Words are valuable tools of communication. Nevertheless, we understand them through the lens of meaning that our culture, time period, and education imbue them with. The universal nature of the Buddha's message is beyond these uncertain and ever-changing partitions. In this book, the goal is not to polish the language into literary or stylized prose, but rather to preserve the author's intention to the best of our understanding. As Karmapa's audience is somewhat knowledgeable—as opposed to being made up of primarily newcomers—he interchanges Sanskrit and Tibetan terms. The translator has systematically included footnotes with translations, references, or explanations to accompany these terms.

We thank the many people who contributed to this work through their support and comments. Our sincere gratitude goes to Alexandra Gonzalez, Andrea Höbart, and Gilles Seigneurgens for the initial transcription, Claudine Ledroit and Marithé Juanchich for their eagle-eyed copyediting, Karma Migyur Ling Center for Tibetan Studies for hosting the event, and the venerable Lama Teunzang.

May Karmapa's words inspire us, guide us, and give each of us a taste of Buddhist practice.

Audrey Desserrières
August 11, 2019

Introduction

If we are taking a class, in some ways, we have the time and space to focus on the subject and its important points more profoundly. When we have the opportunity of gatherings like the present one, one has to find a way to summarize the essential points and at the same time make sure that everyone is able to bring something with him or herself once the event is complete so that everybody has something to practice on. Therefore, please excuse me if I skip the formal procedures or steps that normally should go with the explanations.

It is a great pleasure to be able to share my own understanding of the Buddha's teachings and methods that we call the Buddhadharma. I hope the following few thoughts will benefit you in some ways. It is very inspiring to me to have this sort of opportunity every now and then because of my own devotion and genuine interest in the Dharma.

On a certain relative scale, we are, in some ways, bordered by time, distance, culture, mentality, and language. However, due to almost unimaginable settings or circumstances, we all share the same interest and therefore we are able to come together and practice the Buddhadharma.

Many of you have a strong connection with the Buddhadharma and, out of keen interest and respect, you have spent much time studying it, practicing it, and also doing your best to apply it in your daily lives. I am therefore sure you will understand its benefit.

There is a historical way of describing how Buddhism— whether we call it a religion or a spirituality—came into being in our human history or world. At the same time, from a purely Buddhist point of view, there is a nonlinear way of describing it.

Most of you are familiar with the historical one. More than 2,500 years ago, in the land that we now call Nepal, in Lumbini, the well-known figure of the great Prince Siddhartha was born. To put it very briefly: when he actualized enlightenment, after his realization of the meaning of life, he started to teach his experience to others in response to a request, and this came to be known as the teachings, or Buddha's experience, or Buddhadharma—that is, his wisdom. Over the course of the years until now, we have enjoyed and benefited from the teachings. In short, they can be summarized as the teachings of compassion and loving kindness as well as wisdom.

We all know the historical Buddha, the enlightened being, as the Fourth Buddha, Buddha Shakyamuni. We have practiced his understanding or realization of what life and the meaning of spirituality are about through the present day.

As each universe begins to develop in time, so does the consciousness of sentient beings, particularly that of human beings. They grow, and various forms of spirituality such as this one also begin to grow within them. That is the basis for the birth of Buddhism according to a linear progression.

The nonlinear way to explain it is that, just as there are countless sentient beings, there are countless buddhas as well. Therefore, there is no real way to describe who the first Buddha or the last Buddha is. It is said that as long as there are sentient beings then the activity of the buddhas is always present. It is spontaneously present.

This is linked with the aspirations of those individuals who became enlightened, and the basis for it is none other than compassion and wisdom. Compassion and wisdom automatically generate a kind of wish that makes for their presence. It is the aspiration of enlightened attitude, *bodhichitta*[1] in Sanskrit. In other words, as long as there are sentient beings who need support or help to liberate themselves from causality or karma[2]—and from the change within this causality—and who are equally disturbed by the afflictive emotions (called *kleshas* in Sanskrit[3]), then the buddhas' activity is always present.

This is important to remember and remind ourselves of, particularly when we address the topic of refuge, in Tibet-

---

1   *jangchup semkyé* བྱང་ཆུབ་སེམས་བསྐྱེད། in Tibetan.

2   Causality or karma (ལས་རྒྱུ་འབྲས།) *lé gyümdré* in Tibetan) is the natural process according to which any deed acts as a cause for a future result or consequence. Karmapa explains, "If a seed is planted, it will automatically give its result."

3   *nyönmong* ཉོན་མོངས། in Tibetan.

an known as *kyap su drowa*[4]. Even though we are familiar with this notion, we do need a little bit of a reminder of exactly why we are practicing the refuge.

---

4 སྐྱབས་སུ་འགྲོ་བ། Literally "going under the protection." *Sharana* in Sanskrit.

Seeking Buddhist Refuge

The Motivation for Seeking Refuge

Motivation is important when taking refuge. We are all logic or story oriented. For example, we consider our birth or physical experience as a linear progression. Our mind has thus adapted to that, and therefore one sees, thinks, and communicates in this way. Therefore, the very practice of refuge, which is known as the practice where we take our first step into the ways of the buddhas and bodhisattvas, begins with a kind of motivation. I would use the word *fear* for it, which might be strange. The path to enlightenment is paved not with fear but with devotion, confidence, compassion, and so on, so the word *fear* might sound very contradictory in this context.

The phenomenon, the idea, or the nature of fear is just like any other phenomenon. It cannot be only confined to or absolutely defined as positive or negative. It is just an experience, just another phenomenon. If it is used appropriately, in moderation, then it has its own benefit and quality.

One thing that comes to mind as an analogy for fear is the spice chili. In our cuisine, if there is not a tinge or a touch of spice—it can be any form of spice—the dish somehow loses its vigor, its actual taste. However, you just need the right amount of it.

Another example is poison. For a medicine to actually work, it needs the appropriate amount of poison so that it has a curing quality.

Therefore, it is said that in order to keep the motivation and not to lose its momentum, we need the right amount of fear. Not in a sense that we are completely driven by frightful things, but in a way that there is that tanginess of realization that things are precious, that things are scarce, rare, and impermanent. It is that realization that I would translate as *fear* in a way.

The first instinct that we have is always for ourselves, for our own protection and benefit. When we fall, we will instantly use our limbs to protect ourselves. In the practice of refuge, we begin by having a sense of fear about the fact that we could lose this precious existence, this precious opportunity. It is precious from the point of view that it is very capable—the most fertile soil to plant any seed you wish to plant—yet at the same time, we can lose it at any moment. That kind of healthy part of fear, the right amount of it, gives us the right drive and the motivation to seek the Buddhist path and begin the journey.

Traditionally, the teachings of the Buddhist refuge always

explain that we need to have fear of *samsara*[5] as a foundation. This means that if we give in to disturbing emotions and start to plant unfavorable seeds in our mind by way of actions, speech, and thoughts, then one could lose or obscure one's innate clarity more and more to a point where one becomes quite confident that there is no clarity! That the disturbing aspects of the mind or consciousness are all one has, and one loses one's way to realizing that there is hope. Therefore, the teachings say that we need to have a tinge of fear in a way, so that, to begin with, we refrain from giving in to emotions until our strength grows and we are capable enough to no longer depend on anything because we have actualized complete realization.

A sensible mind or person knows how to use everything in moderation or in the appropriate amount. The circumstances may be different for every individual. For some, it may be very clear that there is simply no distraction in terms of what is happening around. They recognize that we are all standing on a very impermanent and ever-changing ground. Having realized and being comfortable with that fact, one does not need to add any more extra perspective or practice on top of it. Therefore, they can already move from that point onward to the next step.

However, sometimes one eats although the hunger has already been taken care of. One has quenched one's thirst and one has eaten; nevertheless, the habit of continuously munching on things is still present. In the same way, from this point onwards, as a practitioner one normally recognizes and understands what one needs to renounce, to realize, or to acquire. Nevertheless, the idle habit of accumu-

---

5   *korwa* འཁོར་བ། in Tibetan. Samsara refers to the succession of existences infused with the ineluctable suffering of birth, sickness, old age, and death.

lating further additional and unnecessary karma is there. The idea is to know how to utilize various understandings and experiences. In order for some to get motivated into the practice, the traditional way is sufficient—recognizing that there is a risk involved, a danger in a way—that if one does not utilize this very favorable condition, it could be lost anytime, so they need to apply that approach.

Then, without being overwhelmed by it, one makes sure not to lose or waste any time and energy. The individual is thus able to acquire what is known as merit and, together with that, the experience or knowledge we call wisdom.

At the end of course, the aim is to seek that clarity and to reach its perfection; nothing more. However, it can differ according to the individual. There are variations in the practice of the refuge. One is known as the way of the bodhisattvas[6]. Some people may be interested in following it. For them it is far more meaningful or interesting to recognize that not just oneself needs to be benefitted, but all other sentient beings as well. In this case, the caring aspect—the compassionate and loving aspect within ourselves—is such that there is greater awareness. One's instinct of benefitting oneself is still present, but this individual realizes that he or she is in a position where he or she can do something that has never been done before. It is a platform where one can not only acquire that realization for oneself, but for all others as well.

This orientation comes naturally to that individual and is described as one's kind, type, family, or category (rik[7] in Tibetan). We say that the individual has awakened to this

---

6   In Sanskrit; *jangchup sempa* བྱང་ཆུབ་སེམས་དཔའ། in Tibetan.

7   རིགས། *gotra* in Sanskrit.

potential (*rik sepa*[8] in Tibetan). This means that when the conditions are favorable and one's own obscurations have diminished—one's consciousness is calm and composed—it is then the most appropriate moment to realize exactly the kind of fortune one has.

In a nutshell, the point is that the practice of refuge is very general in all forms of Buddhism: to seek the enlightened state, Buddhahood. However, whether it is a practice of refuge according to the way of the bodhisattvas or not is defined by the object of fear. The general way or common refuge is intended for oneself. One sees that the conditions one is in are favorable, yet at the same time they are mixed with a lot of traps, pitfalls, and risks. Therefore, one seeks a way to avoid them and at the same time attain liberation. Whereas, on the bodhisattva path, the same kind of fear is there, but in this case the fear is like that of a parent; fear is not only for oneself, but for others as well.

The kind of refuge we take in our tradition, either for the first time or as a continuous practice, is the way of the bodhisattvas.

In short, the term *bodhisattva* refers to an aspect of our mind we can call consciousness or wisdom—this very aspect of ourselves described earlier as clarity or enlightened state—seeking that same thing, the state of enlightenment, with the purpose to do it not only for one's own benefit, but for others, no matter who they may be or how many they may be.

The example is that of a caring father or mother who has

---

8   རིགས་སད་པ།

no favorite among their loved ones. No matter how many they are or how different they may be in terms of character, personality, age—it does not matter to them. They care for them and love them equally. It is often the case that if one child is more challenging or tough in character than the others, they would care for him or her even more, devoting time and patience to do whatever is necessary in order to help that individual. In short, a very informal way of defining a bodhisattva is to compare him or her to a parent, I suppose.

The practice of refuge serves as both a foundation and the first step towards becoming a bodhisattva. It is also a foundation for all the other practices that come afterwards, for everything we do.

This practice is understood as a vow or an ordination (*dompa*[9] in Tibetan). For some, the term *vow* may have the meaning of confining or restricting oneself to a point where one is not being allowed to be oneself. However, that is definitely not the case here. To my understanding, the vow part is a way, a path, to cultivate what brings calm and composure in oneself. Thus, one realizes that through this path, one keeps a sense of distance from what brings disturbance in him or herself—the disturbing emotions, the *kleshas*. Together with this vow, one then avoids accumulating any more unnecessary karmas. Therefore, it brings a state of clarity and calmness. Thus, it is not a way to shut the door, but to acquire an environment where one can focus on what is most important.

For example, a person who has no knowledge that com-

---

9   སྡོམ་པ། *samvara* in Sanskrit.

passion exists and is real has no other choice but to be dependent and to resolve issues using whatever is at his or her disposal—it could be anger, desire or any other emotions—in order to help oneself and even others too. In this case, what happens when one practices the ways of the bodhisattvas through taking up these precious vows (of course this is a kind of labelling) is that if by fortune that person, who had no knowledge of compassion, happens to understand that something called compassion exists, and sees only a glimpse of its quality, then naturally, without having to say or do anything, the person will automatically renounce all the other disturbing emotions and follow after compassion. That is the practice of the refuge according to the way of the bodhisattvas.

Refuge in the Enlightened State: The Buddha

The object of refuge is obviously none other than the Buddha, or the enlightened state. I suppose most of us relate to it as someone or something, or a name of a person, but the reality is that *buddha* is just a term to describe the quality of a state of consciousness or wisdom, commonly known to us as a state of mind. This state of mind is a phenomenon, an aspect of ourselves that can recognize that it is not obstructed when it is calm, composed, undisturbed, and not dependent on causes and conditions. There is an aspect of ourselves that can recognize everything as it is. We describe that as mind; consciousness—or a very respectful term for it is wisdom.

This may lead us to think that it is a completely independent phenomenon, and that there is something to grasp, something tangible and permanent in a way. Buddha teaches that one way of saying is that it's not that, but another way of saying is that it's more than that. It is beyond that.

To understand what *more than that* or *beyond* means, we can use the example of any experience we make or made. Something closer to what we can relate to is probably anger. It may not be what we expect, but any kind of emotion can be taken as an example or anything we feel inspired about, like the care and loving kindness that we experience from our parents.

From a logical point of view, we can define and describe the object of anger: a cause which ignites the emotion, and then comes the whole effect of it. Nevertheless, if you really carefully examine it, you see that it is actually just a way to define it in terms of logic. What really happened is that when anger comes into being, actually there is no real reason. It just happens, and there is no sort of distinction between "I'm here angry," and "there is an object out there that I am angry at."

The caring, or compassionate and loving, aspect manifests in the same way. Our logical minds need a story with a beginning in terms of a cause and then other various forms of causes that force it to continue, and then finally comes the end, the completion. I suppose the reality is that the compassion and loving kindness just happen by themselves.

Every time that I practice, I try to relate to the teachings. This practice is none other than the practice of compassion, and the traditional method is to focus on the kindness of one's parents and most particularly that of the mother as the one who cares for us from the moment we are conceived. Then, I try to relate it to my own mother, and try to put myself in her place; at least try to imagine. It is quite extraordinary, although it is only imagination. When I look with my own logic, there is no real reason to care for this thing that comes into life. From a logical point of view, the moment that this individual comes into being, he or she would be none other than the cause of all kinds of confusion, headaches, sleepless nights, and worries. Up to this day, my mother is still worrying about me! Therefore, from a logical point of view, this sentient being is not an object of care or love.

Of course, each of us relates to our parents in different ways. Some relate to their biological parents or mother, but for some the parents are a figure, a non-biological one. So each context may vary. Nevertheless, the traditional method is to think particularly of the biological mother. The experience (which I will never know in this life) must be extraordinary. During the many months when the baby stays in the womb, there is a physical experience of not being separate. It's almost as if it is yourself, but at the same time you would care more for this individual than you would care for yourself. From a logical point of view, that just does not make sense. Because from the moment you have that individual growing in you, then to the end of your life, you basically give birth to worries and problems, and your life as you knew it is over.

That parenting aspect of ourselves has no real or linear beginning; it has no real story; it is referenceless—beyond logic and concepts. It just happens. I am sure parents also wonder themselves sometimes why they care so much! But they just do. In their own way of course, but they do. They are used to the concept[10] of thinking *my son* or *my daughter*, but it's just because that's how they were conditioned to

---

10   Karmapa explains that here, the word *concept* is used for ཐ་སྙད། *tanyé* in Tibetan (*vyavahara* in Sanskrit) which usually means *designation, label, concept or idea*.

think. What really happens the moment they worry is that there is no distance, no time, no logic; all the concepts we are used to are all gone, and it happens right there.

Anger also works in that same way as well. Of course, there is the usual context where a social interaction between individuals ignites something and then the anger arises. But sometimes anger is just anger! I am sure all of you have experienced the following (I have had many experiences of it): banging your toe on the corner of the table or the bedpost. It is one of those most indescribable experiences. It's without words and there is a strong emotion coming out of it. Words will be used in order to try to explain the experience and the way it has arisen. Otherwise we cannot describe it. Yet at the same time, in this indescribable moment, the presence of mind is very clear and you see what has happened and how it was caused, but you cannot really put it into words.

The consciousness, state of mind, or phenomenon that is called enlightened state is something like that. What we label buddhahood or the enlightened state is a way of describing that the clarity is complete and has reached its full maturity. That is the object of refuge.

We could very easily misinterpret *taking refuge* in the Buddha, or the expression taking refuge, and think that it is a way to worship a divinity, a higher dimension, a higher being, or something that is superior to us. The meaning of refuge is quite different from that.

There is nothing wrong with worshipping. One might say it is a sort of art, an expression of our interest or enthusiasm. For example, we could worship a tree, in a healthy way, meaning that we care for it; we water it and garden it in such a way that we give it a lot of respect.

However, the practice of refuge, and particularly the refuge in the Buddha, means that there is a practical understanding that comes from a calm state of accepting that, first of all, we do have this quality of clarity, right now. Right now, we have this potential to see things clearly when we are calm and cool. Yet, when this state is disturbed, then it can also change. Therefore, recognizing the quality of the Buddha means seeing that there is proof—a guarantee in a way—that there is a state where this clarity can remain utterly undisturbed. By seeing that, we then become inspired and we gain and generate confidence. It is not about having a display or something that looks like worshipping as a practice, but, deep down, it is this hope, this realization, that we too can obtain or reach that state. That is the real refuge.

It is said that sentient beings are endowed with the potential of buddha nature. Nevertheless, for our mundane view—rather than forcing ourselves to see that in the first place—the very first step is to look towards that enlightened being. Then, naturally, inspiration and respect will arise. That is why the very first practice is to focus and meditate on the qualities of a buddha. This inspiration is what motivates us to be a practitioner, and it drives us to continue on our path and to become an enlightened being ourselves.

Otherwise, we all have our moments of brilliance. I had many moments of brilliance! While I was spending a number of years in a part of India called Kalimpong[11], I was often spending time studying Buddhist scriptures and phi-

---

11 City in the Indian state of West Bengal and location of Diwakar Buddhist Academy—a college for higher Buddhist studies, in addition to a publishing house.

losophy. One night, as I was doing my homework, for some reason I had this sort of moment of brilliance and I suddenly felt, "My goodness! I have unlocked the truth! I'd better write all of this down before I forget it." So I wrote everything as quickly and as clearly as I could, as I thought at the time. I then slept very happily. The next morning when I woke up, I remembered it, and I immediately went to open my notebook. Then I realized that it was all just gibberish actually! What was written there did not make any sense at all! We all have our moments of brilliance.

Through the descriptions or explanations we receive, whether we believe it or not, when we study and meditate on the quality of a buddha, it at least brings the inspiration to our logical and conceptual minds that it is possible to have not only a few moments of brilliance but a clarity that is completely developed and blossomed. Fortunately for us as practitioners, over the many decades, centuries, and millennia up till now we have enjoyed a great many teachers who are proofs of having realized that clarity. We are very fortunate to have that kind of evidence in our era. This helps us not take for granted our existence in this world due to thinking that it just happens by coincidence or circumstance and is merely ordinary and common. It gives us the inspiration to realize that each of us has that potential.

Another description used for a buddha is *perfectly enlightened,* which means that this quality of clarity is fully blossomed and developed. From the very first moment when we try to engage in cultivating that quality as a practitioner, we have to have this courage, this confidence, that in the end, we will ourselves reach the same state and no longer continue to be dependent. Otherwise, we could arrive at a point where we are always dependent on someone or something, and this could very well be the idea of a buddha. The moment we do that—because we believe ourselves to be dependent on something—what really happens is that this *something* we are dependent on has to somehow be dependent on something else, otherwise it can never function and there is no quality and no interaction at all. Therefore, there is a vicious circle.

Refuge in the Path: The Dharma

During the initial period, we depend on the path just so that we are able to understand the quality of clarity that is the undisturbed state of mind to a greater and greater degree. We let go of disturbing emotions and unveil the obscurations (*dripa*[12] in Tibetan) in the forms of unnecessary habits and karma, meaning that first of all one purifies the karma by letting go of whatever has already ripened (it could be in the form of obstacles or of this very existence). We let it be or we let it go, and at the same time the mind does not try to cling to it or crave it and therefore stops planting any more karmic seeds.

Therefore, by depending on the path, the Buddhadharma, and by initially refraining from karma, *kleshas*, and obscurations, one finds out that there is clarity. We are inspired in the first place, but the more we are able to renounce them, the more the clarity reveals itself. As we reach accomplishment, it becomes very natural and effortless until it is a state of perfection.

What we first try to do is understand that all of this is possible. Thus, we begin with a form of ritual or process.

---

12 སྒྲིབ་པ། *avarana* in Sanskrit.

We depend on a tool that is called the Buddhadharma, but towards the end of the path, we realize that we are not forever dependent on something—that we ourselves are *dependentless*. It becomes clear to the wisdom that there is no need, no requirement, to give birth to any other karma from here onwards. The taking of refuge in the Dharma then actually takes place.

First of all, within the scope of our own capacity, it could be utilizing whatever moment one can spare to educate ourselves on and listen to the knowledge or the experience of the buddhas which is known as the Buddhadharma. This is information on the direct experience of a fully conscious mind.

This can begin with the formal education in the Buddhist way, starting with learning the scriptures—the sutras[13] and the *shastras*[14] to begin with and then the tantras[15]. Then, whatever amount of information one has gained, one uses it and applies the Dharma. This means that one reflects to make sure one has understood—not merely heard or listened. It is a threefold learning process known in Tibetan as *tö, sam, gom*[16]. *Tö* means listening, *sam* is re-

---

13 The sutras (*do* མདོ in Tibetan) are the collections of the teachings spoken by the Buddha and transcribed from memory by his first disciples. They primarily concern the training in meditation.

14 The *shastras* (*tentchö* བསྟན་བཅོས། in Tibetan) are the exegesis or commentaries written by spiritual authorities to elucidate the Buddha's teachings and methods after his passing. The Indian *shastras* are included in the Tibetan and Chinese Buddhist Canon.

15 "The Vajrayana teachings were presented by Buddha Vajradhara and preserved in the scriptures known as the 'tantras'. According to most masters, Indian and Tibetan, the tantras themselves may be grouped in four sets: the *kriya*, *charya*, *yoga* and *anuttarayoga* classes of tantras. In terms of locating these tantric scriptures, it is most appropriate to regard the tantras as representing a fourth 'basket' of the Buddha's teaching." In Lama Jampa Thaye. The tantras form the 7th and last section of the Tibetan Canon.

16 ཐོས་བསམ་སྒོམ། *shruta, asaya, bhavana* in Sanskrit.

flecting or contemplating, and *gompa* is meditating or trying to get a direct experience of whatever one has listened to and reflected on.

The practice of those three aspects could start anywhere. As it is said, a bodhisattva must learn anything that is to be known. It could start with the practice of giving or generosity, in Sanskrit known as *dana*[17]. First, we listen carefully to the benefit of giving, and then we reflect on it, making sure that we understand it logically (its benefit; how to give; when to give; what to give). Finally, meditating means that we actually begin with the practice giving.

During our lifetimes, we engage in various activities. Whether we are aware of it or not, we continuously provide, give, and offer things to others. In the same way, we try to complement that art of giving by the support of concentration, clarity, ethics, and so on. The practice of giving is not foreign to us. In fact, it is very natural, and we engage in it every day. If we focus on the moment the day starts, we begin to breathe, and breathing involves automatically inhaling and exhaling. So right there, we start to give already. Then from that moment onwards, whether we pass on any thoughts and comments or generate any kind of activity—no matter how mundane they may be— like for example having a breakfast or a cup of tea, the giving aspect is present. Actually, giving and receiving go together; it is something like an exchange that is there all the time. We simply do not have the habit of realizing it.

The meditation part begins with utilizing what one has reflected upon, in that case giving. A very informal way of

---

17 *jinpa* སྦྱིན་པ། in Tibetan.

starting that meditation consists in taking a bit of time in our daily lives to realize that we are constantly giving and receiving as well (which is basically another way of giving). The formal way is to meditate that we are offering or giving to all sentient beings—however many they are—everything we own or could ever experience or call *mine*. In this case, one could call it one's body, speech, and mind, or the universe, or it could be the formal practice known as the practice of mandala[18], where we offer everything there is to offer. Without involving ourselves in actually, physically engaging in giving anything, we begin by using the ability of our consciousness.

Whatever formal practices we do, they are all practices of giving if you really focus. For example, if you meditate on Chenrezig[19], a light radiates from the heart-syllable towards all sentient beings in all directions; that itself is the practice of giving. In the practice of *tonglen*[20] based on the breath, one part consists of exhaling and, while doing so, meditating that we offer all of one's merit, wisdom, and whatever is most precious, dear to us, and rare. Developing that kind of giving habit or giving heart is itself the practice of giving.

---

18 Third practice of the four uncommon preliminary practices of Vajrayana. This meditative practice aims at accumulating merit by mentally offering or giving whatever one can imagine (one's possessions, body, qualities, etc.)

19 Chenrezig (Avalokitesvara in Sanskrit) is the bodhisattva of compassion and loving-kindness. A meditative practice linked to him exists as a means for the practitioner to reveal the same qualities of compassion and loving-kindness within him or herself.

20 གཏོང་ལེན། "Breath out: *As much compassion and love as I have, as much merit as I have gained, and all good wishes, may it reach every sentient being without exception and bring them happiness*. Breath in: *As much suffering as sentient beings have, may it all, without exception, come into me*. Breathing out is like giving medicine; breathing in is like drawing the poison out of a wound." In Shamar Rinpoche, *The Path to Awakening: How Buddhism's Seven Points of Mind Training Can Lead You to a Life of Enlightenment and Happiness*, p. 90-91.

Refuge in the Way of the Bodhisattvas: The Sangha

In order to supplement the aforementioned practice, we also live concordantly, according to our comfort and our own condition or capacity through the way we think, carry our voice, and physically engage. This is basically known as the practice of ten virtues[21] through our three doors: our body, speech, and mind. We try to develop all of these virtues as much as possible according to our capacities so that they complement and support our practice of giving.

It is not natural to a buddha, an enlightened being, to think nonvirtuous thoughts, to speak and to act nonvirtuously. When we commit ourselves to that kind of conduct and way of living and practice it, each moment we spend is already the same as that of a Buddha. Although relatively we may not be enlightened yet, the same amount of merit is gathered.

In our contemporary era, in some ways, the time may not be favorable for the venerable ordained Sangha to manifest, but we have the fortune that they are still present with us. The benefit of the Sangha is that they ensure that the Buddhadharma and the attaining of Buddhahood are very much alive and present. Finding a way to imitate the venerable Sangha's life or live their life, within our own capacity, will help us immensely. That is very much part of the practice of taking refuge in the Sangha.

Formally going through the rhythm of reciting the text of the practice of refuge in terms of reciting the words—be it in Sanskrit, Pali, Tibetan, or any other languages—on a

---

21 The ten virtues: protecting life, practicing generosity, having respectful sexual conduct, speaking the truth, pacifying disputes, speaking peacefully and politely, speaking meaningfully, fostering few desires and being content, meditating on loving-kindness and other altruistic notions, and adopting a view consistent with reality. See Gampopa.

daily basis has its own immense benefit. But on top of that, if we can engage in the listening part, the contemplating part, the meditating part, and then try to spend whatever amount of time towards that direction, that is actually far more of a practice than just reciting the words.

Therefore, we must realize the kind of opportunity that we have: the knowledge of Dharma is very much available to us. It is just a matter of us learning it and becoming educated in it. At the same time, some individuals are devoted to that particular Buddhadharma and try to follow it in the ways of being ordained, learning the scriptures, or going into long formal meditation retreats. Having them around at this time and era is extremely precious.

It means that there are individuals who see the benefit of Buddhadharma and have the merit—the good karma—and most importantly the enthusiasm (*drowa*[22] in Tibetan). They enjoy practicing it; they enjoy living or spending their time like that. They give us inspiration that the path to seek clarity—enlightenment—is very much present. They are living proof, and this brings a lot of hope.

If we have the opportunity to practice the Buddhadharma in the same way as these individuals, we must make sure that we do our best to do so. If we don't, the most important aspect in the way of the bodhisattva is to appreciate that they are there, to rejoice for them, and never to foster thoughts that such practices are now obsolete and not fitting to our contemporary culture.

The Practice of Refuge

There is a ritual we can rely on on a regular basis; the

---

22 ༏ *utsaha* in Sanskrit.

formal practice. It will help us to remind ourselves of the qualities of the Buddha and not deviate from them. It is like a helping hand that makes sure that we do not lose our balance if we are not used to walking. However, the real refuge takes place when we engage in not just imagining or conceptually focusing on the qualities of a buddha or a bodhisattva, but when, within one's own capacity, we make sure that every day any moment is not lost in terms of applying what we can to be like a bodhisattva or a buddha.

Having said all of that, I think it is important for us to understand the precious opportunity that is ours in the form of realizing that human existence is not unimportant and ordinary, but meaningful and beneficial because of its ability. We are at the doorstep of being able to not only liberate ourselves from karma and disturbing emotions but also all other sentient beings. In a very practical manner, that is within our capacity and understanding.

The mindset is of course very important. We all seek the same thing: not to experience suffering. Therefore, even if it is just for one moment—a few minutes, an hour maximum—one should reflect on the nature of what is known as samsara—the ever-circling, ongoing, endless repetition of doing the same thing without any meaning. One needs to be really practical and honest—no matter how uncomfortable it may be to reflect on its nature—without over-criticizing it, but instead trying to recognize it as it is—how it just revolves around over and over again.

Samsara can be compared to eating: from the moment we are born till today, we have eaten every day, three times a day; maybe less; maybe more. No matter how many times we have eaten, we are never full. It is the same thing with rebirth. We have done this many times, not just a few rebirths but for countless and beginningless rebirths.

The Tibetan representation of the wheel of life is interesting to have a look at. It shows an animal like a giant frog with fangs—basically like a reptile—and then the whole wheel of life with birth and death and, in between, the living conditions and the various of realms of existence[23] all presented there. The wheel is an ongoing one. It is actually in the mouth of the animal. One has already gone through all of the cycle of those different realms. We have been at the top, in the middle, and at the bottom. We have been going up and down all the time, but it was never really satisfying. There was never a moment where we really felt that we were finally content. That is samsara.

Considering this may bring an uncomfortable or unpleasant feeling. It may also bring humor and all sorts of experiences. It is worthwhile to take some time to focus on the fact that it is a state where one is never ever content. In doing so, we generate a mindset that is like the agent making the soil fertile. Thus, it automatically becomes suitable to seek the obtaining of the qualities of the Buddha.

To further add on to this topic, it is not a hallucination or an illusion that we are trying to focus on. In fact, it is a reality that within the timeframe of our human experience—no matter the number of years it may be—we could be on top of the world in the morning—enjoying the most amazing and elaborate breakfast and eating like kings—and then in the evening not even have a glass of water to drink. Every minute, hour, day, and week, we constantly

---

23 The Buddha explains six different realms of existence in his teaching: the divine, semidivine, human, animal, hungry ghosts, and hellish realms. Among those six, only the human and animal realms are perceptible by a human being.

experience these different states—being on top of the world, at its bottom, or in between, in a sort of no man's land. Wherever we are, we are never content. The moment we are on top, we are not content and begin to probably envy the lesser. And obviously, when we are not on the top of the world, we always envy that part of the world, that part of life. It is a reality that is happening all the time. Therefore, just taking a moment to reflect on that gives us a kind of realistic overview of where we are.

With that kind of mindset, we should then seek to utilize this moment to take refuge in the Buddha, Dharma, and Sangha for the sake of all sentient beings.

Then we have a moment of freedom. It is an opportunity we have. For some it is like a glimpse, because we have calmed the mind to such a point that we can be in a state of great equanimity, meaning that we are not consumed, bothered, or itched by any of the "worldly *dharmas*[24]." This means that we are able to utilize this moment to let go of the common factors such as pleasant/unpleasant; good/ bad; friends/foes; top/bottom; all those various extreme opposites. This moment may be very brief. Nevertheless, it is one of the most profound moments in our life because we let go of it all and we simply focus on seeing all others as a reflection of oneself, for example.

We all, almost naturally, innately, have a very noble, re-spectable, decent image of ourselves—no matter what we think of ourselves; no matter our culture, profession, or mentality. Therefore, we can use this moment to see all oth-ers as one's own reflection and without any differences of any kind, to see all as the same. We use that kind of attitude.

---

24 Also called the eight worldly concerns, mundane preoccupations, or obsessions *jikten chö gyé* འཇིག་རྟེན་ཆོས་བརྒྱད།: hope for happiness and fear of suffering; hope for gain and fear of loss; hope for praise and fear of blame; hope for fame and fear of insignificance.

For everyone's sake then, we meditate that the buddhas of the ten directions are very much present in this moment with us in the form of the historical Shakyamuni Buddha, the Fourth Buddha. Together with him, the Buddhadharma is also very much present in our time and era—like a reference, an object of devotion for the understanding, the wisdom, or wishes of the Buddha. Thus, we meditate countless Buddhadharma texts behind Buddha Shakyamuni's form. Then, around the Buddha and Dharma texts, we meditate countless forms of Chenrezig, not just a few millions or billions, but countless, as many as one can imagine. These three aspects of refuge are displayed on what is known as the wish-fulfilling tree.

We meditate ourselves in front of that immense tree flanked by all sentient beings—everyone we can imagine, relate to, know, or don't know—however and whoever they might be. Then we recite the words of the prayer, invocation.

སངས་རྒྱས་ཆོས་དང་ཚོགས་ཀྱི་མཆོག་རྣམས་ལ།
sangyé chö dang tsok kyi chok nam la

བྱང་ཆུབ་བར་དུ་བདག་ནི་སྐྱབས་སུ་མཆི།
changchup bardu daknyi kyap su chi

བདག་གིས་སྦྱིན་སོགས་བགྱིས་པའི་བསོད་ནམས་ཀྱིས།
dak gyi jin sok gyi pé sönam kyi

འགྲོ་ལ་ཕན་ཕྱིར་སངས་རྒྱས་འགྲུབ་པར་ཤོག
dro la pen chir sangyé drup par sho

> *To the Buddha, Dharma, and the supreme community*
> *I go for refuge until enlightenment*

*Through the merit of having practiced generosity and the other
[paramitas]*

May enlightenment be achieved for the sake of living beings.[25]

Although we are repeating the words, taking refuge does
not mean *I am a Buddhist* because that is just a label. It
means that because of my devotion—my genuine interest—from here onwards, I would like to think, say, and do
nothing more than what the buddhas and bodhisattvas do.
With that kind of understanding, we acknowledge that we
are upholding this vow. We can take a few moments for
ourselves to reflect on it if we need to.

If one has a complete disinterest or gives up this conduct
or breaches it by engaging in the ten non-virtues[26], then
the vow becomes invalid, but until then (and the end of
this rebirth), the vow is very much present, and the merit
will continue to be generated. The way bodhisattvas conduct their lives and generate bodhichitta is emphasized as
the way to maintain this commitment.

We must make a point to use a certain part of our time,
preferably once in the morning and once in the evening, to
repeat these words. They are very short and simple, so it is
very manageable. Therefore, it is very important that we
use those moments to recite it—first maybe in Tibetan,
Sanskrit or Pali, but then afterwards you can read the

---

25 At the time of the teaching, Karmapa formulated the ritual and the words for taking refuge
the first time, which the audience then repeated. In the context of a practical book, it has
been replaced by the typical refuge prayer that one can recite.

26 The ten nonvirtues: (three with respect to the body) taking life; stealing; engaging in sexual
misconduct; (four with respect to speech) lying; speaking divisive words; speaking harsh
words; engaging in idle talk; (three with respect to the mind) fostering covetousness; har-
boring harmful thoughts; maintaining wrong views. For further details, see Gampopa.

translation as well, so that you have an understanding of it. Then meditate and reflect a little on that.

Understanding the meaning will bring enthusiasm, and we will enjoy going through the practice. If you do not understand it yet, you can make prayers and aspirations that in time you will come to understand it. The most important thing is to keep doing it. Whether we are doing it the right way or the wrong way—fortunately there is no real wrong way—whether we have a greater understanding or not; in the end we need to keep doing it. We need to have a continuous rhythm.

By continuously having momentum, a kind of connection, relationship, is built over time. It can be compared to parents who may not have enough experience in parenting; nevertheless they will continue to parent, regardless of whether they know it well or not. At the end of the day, this is what stays, what gives strength in a way.

My teacher, Professor Sempa Dorje[27], gets asked many questions about the Buddhadharma. In the end, his answer is that if we understand it, of course, there is immense benefit, but he insists on the practice part. He sums things up by saying that "more than the knowing is the doing."

---

27 Professor Sempa Dorje is an eminent professor in Buddhist philosophy and Sanskrit, who used to teach at the University of Varanasi, until the 14th Shamar Rinpoche requested him to take part in the education of the then-young 17th Karmapa and teach at Diwakar Buddhist Academy in Kalimpong, India.

Bodhichitta: Enlightened Attitude

Starting with Enthusiasm

Bodhichitta is a Sanskrit term loosely translated into English as "enlightened mind" or "wisdom". A bodhisattva refers to anyone who has taken a genuine interest in that enlightened, clear, and practical attitude. The *ways of the bodhisattvas* means the way that person, once he or she has generated that attitude, goes about his or her daily life. In terms of human existence, the bodhisattvas are equal and the same as us; they have to go about all their daily business just like ourselves. So, how do they get up? How do they go about their day? How do they sleep? How do they think? How do they interact? For the moment, we are trying to touch the surface of the ways of the bodhisattva, so touching the core in reality might take some time. Therefore, what we are trying to do first is to get a glimpse of what it means and, at the same time, if we are interested in the ways of the bodhisattvas, then to see how we go about it.

The Buddhadharma is such that it can be explained in various ways according to our capacity, our motivation, and our interest. Therefore, if we wish for it to be serious, according to the way we grew up and were educated, which was such that we need to feel that there is something serious happening in our lives and that there is a final destination, the Buddhadharma has that quality of adjusting exactly to our wish. On the other hand, if we are keener on the inspiration side and not totally consumed by the seriousness of life, thinking that not everything is hardship or work—not saying that it is all play either— but that there is something wonderful and joyful about it, then the Buddhadharma can provide exactly that. The question is thus, "Which way should we go about it?" I suspect probably the latter one. In fact, the bodhisattva way or the practice of the Buddhadharma is one of the least challenging, the easiest, and simplest ways to understand what everything is about. Shamar Rinpoche[28] used to say that the way of the bodhisattva is such that one will progress from one level of realization to the next just by enjoying it.

It doesn't demand anything really hard; no physical nor mental strain at all. It is said that there are in fact oceans (meaning countless numbers) of means that are beyond the world, which a bodhisattva deploys. They are known as the *paramitas*[29], the perfections. For example, the six paramitas that we often hear about—the perfections of generosity, ethical conduct, patience, joyful effort, meditation, and discernment—or the ten paramitas[30] are means or methods that do not require any strain on ourselves at all.

---

28 Mipham Chökyi Lodrö, the 14th Kunzig Shamarpa (1952–2014).

29 In Sanskrit; *paröl du tchinpa* ཕ་རོལ་ཏུ་ཕྱིན་པ། In Tibetan.

30 The following four are added to the six previous ones: skillful means, aspiration, power, and wisdom.

Let's take as an example the practice of aspiration called *mönlam*[31] in Tibetan. Really focusing on the practice doesn't require us to even lift a finger in a way! All it requires is just using what is most common to us. Every day we make countless wishes, probably not very clear wishes, but at least we all wish, and wishing is very common and natural to us. What the bodhisattvas do is that they utilize this natural expression of ourselves and turn it into something beyond our ordinary concepts, known as *paramita* or *beyond the world*.

There is the condensed and summarized practice of aspiration prayers that we normally recite in our daily prayers or the Kagyü Mönlam[32] in particular during which the *Samantabhadra Aspiration Prayer*[33] is recited. Simply by reading it, one sees one beautiful wish after another.

I say beautiful because it is not really serious, which doesn't mean that it's just by the bye also. It is both not serious and genuine, very honest, and pure, and therefore it is beautiful. We can say that it is not serious because when bodhisattvas make aspirations, they are not concerned, worried, or bothered by the success of this aspiration. One does it because one has immense enthusiasm—not an enthusiasm coming out of effort. As a beginner, we of course need a little bit of effort, but the real enthusiasm comes when it is natural to us. We do not need to force ourselves to breathe. We breathe naturally. We do not need to force ourselves to make our hearts beat. They just

---

31 སྨོན་ལམ། *pranidhana* in Sanskrit.

32 The Kagyü Mönlam བཀའ་བརྒྱུད་སྨོན་ལམ། is an annual prayer gathering in Bodh Gaya, India, at the very place Shakyamuni became the Buddha. During a week, all the Karma Kagyü practitioners gather to recite aspiration prayers for the benefit of all sentient beings. See *The Gate of Two Merits: Prayer Compilation of the Grand Kagyud Monlam.*

33 For a translation of the prayer together with some explanations, see Shamar Rinpoche, *The King of Prayers.*

do. In the same way, real aspiration is natural and spontaneous. When bodhisattvas make aspirations, they are not really bothered whether they are mundane or not, whether they may be too formal or too informal, whether they are doing it the right way or the wrong way, whether they are beautiful or not; they just enjoy making them.

Just like the aspirations, the practice—the means, the ways, and the activity itself—of a bodhisattva can come in countless of forms. For example, you can read about the great numbers of teachers[34] of a bodhisattva called Sudhana[35], the son of a merchant who travelled to various places a long time ago when he was seeking teachers who could convey the means to be able to generate bodhichitta and perfect this enlightened attitude. Along the way, up until he met his final teacher, he met countless teachers, each of them very unique. None of them corresponds to the conventional idea of a teacher or a guide. They are not completely formal ones—not sitting on a throne, dictating every term, directing and delegating this and that, but they come in various forms. Each of them is more fascinating than the last. To name only a few, one teacher he met, Utpalabhuti[36], was constantly doing one single thing, both as a livelihood as well as a practice: acquiring the art of making incense—from gathering the herbs, to putting together the incense sticks or powders, to lighting it. It was his whole practice as well as his livelihood for all his life.

---

34 See the *Gaṇḍavyūhasūtra*. This sutra retraces the Buddhist journey of Sudhana on his quest to enlightenment as he set out to receive instructions from fifty-three spiritual masters. At the very last stage of this quest that is more of an inner journey than an actual outer pilgrimage, he met with the bodhisattva Samantabhadra. The well-known *Samantabhadra Aspiration Prayer* is drawn from this sutra.

35 *tsongpön gyi bu norzang* ཚོང་དཔོན་གྱི་བུ་ནོར་བཟངས། in Tibetan.

36 For the meeting with the perfumer Utpalabhuti, see Cleary p.1258.

Solely through the simple activity of burning one stick of incense, he was able to explain and describe how one can accumulate merit and wisdom.

Another teacher that Sudhana met was actually a ten-year-old child, Indriyeshvara[37]. He was surrounded by thousands of other children playing with him in the sand. In the scripture, the setting almost looks like a mandala of children. Just through his play, this child was able to describe the whole path and practice of the way of the bodhisattvas.

In the same way, we cannot really disregard any act or activity because for a bodhisattva each of them can be transformed, utilized, or channeled in a way that is virtuous and beneficial. Of course, if something is very unpleasant and destructive, we don't need spirituality to inform us that it is harmful. As long as our mind is clear, conscious, and calm—no matter who we are—we will be able to recognize what is improper. For example, if there is actual violence—be it physical or mental—the person will be able to recognize it, directly or indirectly. If fear is used in the most extreme way, and it is deployed in a way that it is unhealthy, everyone can recognize it.

Besides, it is said that a bodhisattva must know everything because any knowledge can be beneficial. Therefore, some of my teachers used to say that we cannot really judge whether such and such profession or post is unfitting or unbeneficial for society. The leaders of a country—politicians, prime ministers, presidents, mayors, heads of a family, etc.—the larger the responsibility, the greater the dis-

---

37 For the meeting with the boy Indriyeshvara, see Cleary p.1229.

cipline, courage, and guts one needs to have. It takes great doing. It is actually something we cannot really imagine if we compare with ourselves. Therefore, my teachers say that we never know who a bodhisattva could be. I am sure they didn't mean the words *courage* and *guts* in a drill fashion where one has to just power through or walk through a wall type of thing. The meaning involves considering that they have great decisions lined up one after another, so their whole day is completely filled with various forms of decisions they need to make. It takes courage that they, too, have to be enthusiastic about what they do and enjoy it—in a healthy way of course. Otherwise, at some point there will be a sense of breakdown.

At times, I enjoy cooking. Simply preparing a meal for oneself involves some degree of organization. Then, when I try to think of the chef of a big restaurant who has to cater and prepare hundreds of dishes, I see that the kind of calm that is required doesn't come from only a few years of practice. They have to go through hours and hours of doing the very same thing and to follow the same routine every day. They need some sense of clarity and enthusiasm for that. Otherwise they will not be able to carry on. I used to be fascinated with it.

When enthusiasm is present in whatever profession, work, or activity we engage in, then we are not truly bothered by doubts or expectations.

This reminds me of the day I learnt how to pour water in a delicate jug. I was sort of in two minds as to whether I should pour it straight in or gently, where I should stop, and how I should balance myself. My mother was there in the kitchen. She had folded her arms and was just observing the whole thing. She didn't say a word of course. She was just observing and, as is often the case, the more you feel that you are being observed, the more nervous you get, and whatever doubts you may have amplify! After some time, my hands were literally shaking, and of course I made a mess! Then, when it came to the second time to refill the jug, she came over, just took it and said, "You just have to do it in one breath and don't doubt. Just do it because if you are going to get it wrong, if you are going to spill it, you are going to spill it anyway! So you might as well do it, and you will learn something if you spill it."

The great bodhisattvas—or any people who really enjoy what they are doing—don't really hesitate so much. There can be a habit of hesitating, but they are not completely overburdened by the hesitation.

I forgot that there was a third person in the kitchen. That was my father, of course. He was also watching both of us interacting. I happened to look at him and of course he didn't say anything, but he had a look that said everything.

Reaching Compassion

I suppose one can begin with the concept of compassion. I use the word concept because when you first begin—in a very practical sense—even if you are touching what is called absolute truth, it is just too far and too distant. The only "tangible" thing a beginner has is a concept. Therefore, I am referring here to the conceptual part of compassion. If there is genuine enthusiasm in something we do, compassion will be almost simultaneously present, like a companion, in the form of this enthusiasm.

For example, an enthusiastic gardener tending plants or

a caring parent nurturing young ones is actually in the moment. They don't have a plan or an organization. They don't really have awareness in a way. Of course, we emphasize that awareness is very important, that the state of enlightenment is complete awareness, but the kind of enthusiasm that they have is not a forced awareness, but just a natural clarity. In that moment of attending to the plant or the child, they don't really have a thought or a presence reminding them, "I am here, the one who attends or looks after, and the object of my interest is in front of me, and now I am doing this or that." Everything just goes flawlessly and naturally.

In the same way, if we are interested in the way of the bodhisattvas, the fundamental thing we have to do in the first place is to understand why these individuals enjoy and are enthusiastic about what they do. Some understanding is needed prior to forcing our way into it. Shantideva's[38] *Bodhicaryavatara*[39], known as *The Way of the Bodhisattva*, is an extensive explanation and guide on how a bodhisattva behaves, thinks, and goes about his or her daily life. It shows what he or she is most enthusiastic about or interested in. Just brushing through that book automatically commands respect and brings inspiration. Something in us becomes moist and melts.

What the bodhisattvas are most interested in and enthusiastic about is a really grounded experience of reality— the loving and caring nature of sentient beings. This caring aspect in an individual is the most stable and strong foundation to build anything on. When that compassionate

---

38 Indian scholar from the 7th century C.E. (His dates of birth and death are approximate).

39 Title in Sanskrit. *jangchup sempé chöpa la juk pa* བྱང་ཆུབ་སེམས་དཔའི་སྤྱོད་པ་ལ་འཇུག་པ། in Tibetan. See Shantideva.

quality is present, not obscured, and expressed, then the person is willing to do anything, even if it is not in his or her interest, even if it is not really his or her cup of tea. The bodhisattvas are willing to learn that and go through challenges without seeing them as a burden.

For example, if a bodhisattva needs to learn the most elaborate and complicated philosophies, spirituality, meditative absorption (*samadhi*[40] in Sanskrit) or anything, he or she will be willing and interested. They will learn your language; your habits; your sport; the kind of cuisine or weather you like; down to the last detail. That is the reason why it is said that compassion and loving kindness are the basis for all merits and all wisdom: it is the basis for respecting causality. It gives room to let go of hindrances, and one is able to accomplish anything.

In the Buddhadharma, both the practices of compassion as well as of primordial wisdom are equally highly emphasized, but, in the end, it is always said that the first and most important thing an individual needs to begin with is compassion. Wisdom can be accumulated later. Compassion gives way to everything.

Compassion is praised and venerated by all buddhas and bodhisattvas. The bodhisattva Chandrakirti[41] begins his teaching *Introduction to the Middle Way*, the *Madhyamaka-vatara*, by praising compassion:

The Shravakas and those halfway to buddhahood are born from the Mighty Sage

---

40 *ting ngé dzin* ཏིང་ངེ་འཛིན། in Tibetan.

41 (7th century C.E.) Indian philosopher and proponent of the Madhyamaka school of thought. More specifically, he established and systematised the Madhyamaka Prasangika method of refutation.

And Buddhas take their birth from Bodhisattva heroes.
Compassion, nonduality, the wish for buddhahood for other's
sake
Are causes of the children of the Conqueror.

Of buddhahood's abundant crop, compassion is the seed.
It is like moisture bringing increase and is said
To ripen in the state of lasting happiness.
Therefore, to begin, I celebrate compassion.[42]

This caring quality and nature that is called compassion
gives birth to the most profound virtuous beings in this
universe: arhats, bodhisattvas, and buddhas. Therefore,
prior to offering any kind of homage or prostrations—
which are the highest form of offering and respect—to anyone or anything else, he first pays homage to the quality
of compassion.

As long as there is compassion, we need not worry or be
over-the-top concerned that we may be handicapped because there is lack of wisdom. In fact, as long as there is
genuine loving kindness, the most practical form of wisdom is naturally present. In very informal terms, wisdom
means intelligence, smartness, in its most natural form. It
is not taught nor forced, and we are not imitating anything. The moment we genuinely care is the most natural
form of intelligence. There is no stupidity from any angle.
Therefore, we have simultaneously generated wisdom.

---

42 ཉན་ཐོས་སངས་རྒྱས་འབྲིང་རྣམས་ཐུབ་དབང་སྐྱེས། སངས་རྒྱས་ཉུང་རྒྱལ་སེམས་དཔའ་ལས་འཁྲུངས་ཤིང་། སྙིང་རྗེའི་སེམས་དང་གཉིས་སུ་མེད་བློ་དང་། བྱང་ཆུབ་སེམས་ནི་རྒྱལ་སྲས་རྣམས་ཀྱི་རྒྱུ། གང་ཕྱིར་བརྩེ་ཉིད་རྒྱལ་བའི་ལོ་ཏོག་ ཕུན་ཚོགས་འདིའི། ས་བོན་དང་ནི་སྤེལ་ལ་ཆུ་འདྲ་ཡུན་རིང་དུ། ཡོངས་སྤྱོད་གནས་ལ་སྨིན་པ་ལྟ་བུར་འདོད་གྱུར་པ། དེ་ཕྱིར་བདག་གིས་ཐོག་མར་སྙིང་རྗེ་བསྟོད་པར་བགྱི། Translation from Chandrakirti, Jamgön Mipham, p.59.

From this point, we can begin to get more and more used to the concept of bodhichitta and of the bodhisattva way. We do not really perfect our concept, but at least we have a more balanced and clearer concept so that we have the right tool to touch reality.

Reading these words may be one-way traffic, yet it is nevertheless a form of communication because whatever is conveyed here can be reflected upon and understood. We have no other way to touch the reality of compassion other than using the form of communication we have—the ideas, terminology, and mental pictures we are used to. Out of their great compassion, the countless buddhas and bodhisattvas have put together the most beneficial concepts, which means that they delivered the actual or absolute truth to us in the form of these concepts, thoughts, or words, so that we are able to utilize them to communicate with each other, remind each other, and tap into something that we can all touch. Of course, saying that doesn't mean that we are not touching reality at all. In fact, we do experience the absolute truth, but somehow, we are not that observant of it, and we do not recognize it. All the great bodhisattvas always insist on this, saying that there is nothing to praise and nothing to criticize, that everything is equal. That is also part of the practice.

I sometimes think that our bodies are in some ways far more intelligent than our minds! If it's hot, it's hot; if it's cold, it's cold; if it's hungry, it's hungry. It is very direct. If you think in this way, our current state of mind is also equally honest and direct. At the right distance from whatever causes and conditions, the mind will react accordingly. This is the clarity mentioned earlier. It is the quality of natural recognition. This is not built, put together, or taught.

The Buddhadharma, the bodhisattva way, or the Buddha's way—no matter how we label it—is a profound and correct concept—in other words a perfect concept or perfect speech. The absolute truth or the absolute part of the Dharma itself doesn't need any interpretation or any kind of tool. For example, when Tilopa just took off his slippers and whacked them on Naropa's head, that was it[43]. Nothing more was needed; no translation nor explanations as to why he hit him. Tilopa just hit him, which led Naropa to realize. If the individual's consciousness is at its most mature state, so that he or she has a very good idea of the concepts, is well aware of and recognizes the compass that is very much pointing towards the absolute—the reality—then anything, even the most mundane event, can give them the very same recognition of the nature of mind.

Therefore, we should not think that we are not mature enough or just beginners and feel disheartened or too far from our destination and lose our inspiration. In fact, we should be a bodhisattva by accepting that at least we are at the doorstep of something wonderful, and rejoice in it, be proud of it, and make sure that we do not lose this enthusiasm.

This enthusiasm is the very merit or force that brings us all together. This journey that we have undertaken—is it enjoyable and pleasant? Does it bring happiness? Probably there isn't a real answer to that. Nevertheless, we all identify that there is something profound and meaningful, and I recognize that as genuine enthusiasm. It is devotion; it is caring. Caring doesn't mean caring for the lineage, but re-

---

43 For the full story of Tilopa and Naropa, two of the eighty-four accomplished practitioners of ancient India and forefathers of the transmission of specific Buddhist methods—particularly in Tibet and in the Karma Kagyü school—see Abhayadatta, p.93.

specting and practicing the Buddhadharma is another way of saying, "I care for sentient beings."

The most realistic and approachable beginning is to start with having compassion for ourselves. Recognizing that we have a compassionate nature—in other words the potential to become a Buddha—called buddha nature or bodhichitta, automatically makes us have respect for ourselves in a way that we will not just refrain from but naturally let go of kleshas and renounce karma without having to be told, forced, or chased after for it. If I am able to liberate this one sentient being to begin with, that is as good as liberating all sentient beings because it is part of the process and part of the practice. If this first sentient being—myself—develops, then this being is capable of benefitting all others.

One could wonder, "Isn't that contradictory? In the end, it looks like having too much respect for oneself is just another way to develop one's ego!" In some ways, that is true. However, it is actually a way to utilize ego, just like fear, as we mentioned earlier. A good, experienced doctor is able to use the right amount of poison to make sure it is the most beneficial medicine. In the same way, if we know how to utilize anything, then we have the freedom to utilize the ego in the most beneficial manner—to take pride in recognizing that giving in to accumulating unfavorable karma and to expressing or engaging in kleshas is beneath us.

Committing to Bodhichitta

When we repeat the words in Tibetan to generate enlightened attitude, the object of respect, devotion, and our most profound witnesses are none other than the Three Jewels:

the Buddha, the Dharma, and the Sangha.

Meditate a universe that is as large as the entirety of space. Then, at the center, meditate an equally large tree. If you are innovative, you can imagine it in your own way. At the center of it, you meditate the Buddha Shakyamuni as large as the universe. If possible, try to meditate that he is the actual living, breathing Buddha rather than a statue or a painting. Probably the closest replica of the Buddha is the one we see in Bodhgaya in the Mahabodhi temple. Behind the Buddha, meditate Dharma texts again in the traditional format we call *puti*[44]—beautifully decorated and as large as the universe as well. On top of each of the remaining branches and leaves, meditate countless four-armed bodhisattva Chenrezigs, both as large and as small as the universe.

In front of that tree, we, ourselves, stand together with all sentient beings assembled behind us. We all take refuge in the Buddha, Dharma, and Sangha. We recognize that although the Three Jewels are precious and always present wherever there are sentient beings, so long as obscurations veil sentient beings' minds, it is almost impossible for them to appear. Yet the buddhas and bodhisattvas manage to find a way to manifest. Therefore, it is not just rare, but it is in fact impossible! One could call them the three impossibles.

Taking refuge in the Sangha means that we always take guidance and pieces of advice from the venerable Sangha—the realized bodhisattvas like Chenrezig who manifest in this world in various forms. It sounds like saying they manifest in mysterious ways, but it actually means in the form of teachers: parents, kindergarten teachers, and all other teachers. The most important in this life is the

---

44 པུ་སྟི།

spiritual teacher—the one who introduces us not only to the notion but to the fact that there is a way to become a buddha, meaning the Buddhadharma. That is the meaning of recognizing the Three Jewels and their preciousness.

In front of these objects of great respect, we commit, lift, develop, or cultivate ourselves in the ways of the bodhisattvas. It signifies that we take up the bodhisattva vow. Unlike the vows for individual liberation[45], the bodhichitta commitment is a vow of attitude. We are trying to develop a compassionate attitude. Even though we may currently relate to it in a conceptual way, our aim and motivation is to touch absolute compassion. The traditional metaphor is the genuine care and love a mother has for her only child. We are trying to utilize this opportunity we call *precious human existence* to give a start to this precious attitude.

Utilize a moment to reflect on the object of your compassion in life. It could be your father, your mother, a sibling, a child, a friend, or a companion. It could be anyone you care for and who also cared and cares for you. Then, do not deviate from there—not over-thinking it, nor under-thinking it, but just remain there.

The words to take up the vow of the bodhisattvas mean that from this moment onward, I will follow the footsteps of the buddhas and bodhisattvas. In exactly the same way as they generated compassion, so will I. They developed wisdom, and I will do the same—not harming anyone including myself—physically, verbally or mentally. On top

---

45 *pratimoksha* in Sanskrit; *sosor tarpé dompa* སོ་སོར་ཐར་པའི་སྡོམ་པ། in Tibetan. Commitments that constitute the essence of the ethical conduct necessary to eliminate behaviors leading to suffering. It consists in refraining from certain actions (at the level of body and speech). Specific commitments are intended for lay practitioners and others for monastic ones.

of that, from now onwards, every activity, speech, and thought will aim at the benefit of all sentient beings, no matter how mundane they are. Then—just like the buddhas and bodhisattvas—I will begin to apply the practices of giving, aspiring, and developing proper conduct, and all the other steps. The most important is the motivation. The aim is the benefit of all sentient beings. Up until I gain enlightenment, I will always take refuge in Buddha, Dharma, and Sangha.

བྱང་ཆུབ་སྙིང་པོར་མཆིས་ཀྱི་བར།

jangchup nyingpor tchi kyi bar

སངས་རྒྱས་རྣམས་ལ་སྐྱབས་སུ་མཆི།

sangyé nam la kyap su chi

ཆོས་དང་བྱང་ཆུབ་སེམས་དཔའ་ཡི།

chö dang jangchup sempa yi

ཚོགས་ལའང་དེ་བཞིན་སྐྱབས་སུ་མཆི།

tsok la'ang dézhin kyap su chi

> *Until the essence of enlightenment is reached,*
> *I go for refuge to the Buddhas.*
> *Also I take refuge in the Dharma and in all the host of*
> *Bodhisattvas.* [46]

ཇི་ལྟར་སྔོན་གྱི་བདེ་གཤེགས་ཀྱིས།

jitar ngön gyi déshek kyi

---

46 This stanza is drawn from the second chapter, "Confession," in the *Bodhicaryavatara* by Shantideva. Translation from Shantideva, p.66, stanza 26.

བྱང་ཆུབ་ཐུགས་ནི་བསྐྱེད་པ་དང་།
jangchup tuk ni kyépa dang

བྱང་ཆུབ་སེམས་དཔའི་བསླབ་པ་ལ།
jangchup sempé lap pa la

དེ་དག་རིམ་བཞིན་གནས་པ་ལྟར།
dédak rim zhin népa tar

དེ་བཞིན་འགྲོ་ལ་ཕན་དོན་དུ།
dézhin dro la pendön du

བྱང་ཆུབ་སེམས་ནི་བསྐྱེད་བགྱི་ཞིང་།
jangchup sem ni kyé gyi zhing

དེ་བཞིན་དུ་ནི་བསླབ་པ་ལའང་།
dézhin du ni lap pa la'ang

རིམ་པ་བཞིན་དུ་བསླབ་པར་བགྱི།
rimpa zhin du lap par gyi

> *Just as all the Buddhas of the past*
> *Have brought forth the awakened mind,*
> *And in the precepts of the Bodhisattvas*
> *Step-by-step abode and trained,*
>
> *Likewise, for the benefit of beings,*
> *I will bring to birth the awakened mind,*
> *And in those precepts, step-by-step,*
> *I will abide and train myself.*[47]

---

47 *Op. cit.* Chapter Three, "Taking hold of Bodhichitta," p.83-84, stanzas 23-24.

After that comes the concluding part—words to rejoice both for oneself and for all sentient beings. As in the practice of refuge, we acknowledge that we have generated bodhichitta. With this acknowledgement, the practice comes to life and becomes real, authentic, and complete. We can play a tape recorder or a digital computer to repeat the words of this Buddhadharma, but it cannot acknowledge it, so it can never be complete. Because of our consciousness—this indescribable nature—we are able to acknowledge it. The moment we recognize it—from there onward until we reach enlightenment—the merit will continue to accumulate forever. As Shantideva says in the *Bodhicaryavatara*:

> *A great and unremitting stream,*
> *A strength of wholesome merit,*
> *Even during sleep and inattention,*
> *Rises equal to the vastness of the sky.*[48]

We can thus take a moment for ourselves to meditate and to recognize it.

After that, we repeat the words to rejoice for ourselves and sentient beings because we are now carrying the name of the bodhisattvas.

དེང་དུས་བདག་ཚེ་འབྲས་བུ་ཡོད།
dengdü dak tsé drébu yö

---

48 *Op. cit.* Chapter One, "The Excellence of Bodhichitta," p.56, stanza 19. དེ་ནས་བཟུང་སྟེ་གཉིད་ ལོག་གམ། །བག་མེད་གྱུར་ཀྱང་བསོད་ནམས་ཤུགས། །རྒྱུན་མི་ཆད་པ་དུ་མ་ཞིག །ནམ་མཁའ་མཉམ་པར་རབ་ཏུ་འབྱུང་།

མི་ཡི་སྲིད་པ་ལེགས་པར་ཐོབ།
mi'i sipa lekpar top

དེ་རིང་སངས་རྒྱས་རིགས་སུ་སྐྱེས།
déring sangyé rik su kyé

སངས་རྒྱས་སྲས་སུ་བདག་དེང་གྱུར།
sangyé sé su dak deng gyur

ད་ནི་བདག་གིས་ཅི་ནས་ཀྱང་།
da ni dak gyi chi né kyang

རིགས་དང་མཐུན་པའི་ལས་བཙམས་ཏེ།
rik dang tünpé lé tsam té

སྐྱོན་མེད་བཙུན་པའི་རིགས་འདི་ལ།
kyön mé tsünpé rik di la

རྙོག་པར་མི་འགྱུར་དེ་ལྟར་བྱ།
nyokpar mingyur détar cha

> Today my life has given fruit.
> This human state has now been well assumed.
> Today I take my birth in Buddha's line,
> And have become the Buddha's child and heir.
> *[...]*
> In every way, then, I will undertake
> Activities befitting such a rank
> And I will do no act to mar
> Or compromise this high and faultless lineage.[49]

---

49 *Op. cit.* Chapter Three, "Taking hold of Bodhichitta", p.84, stanzas 26-27.

བདག་གིས་དེ་རིང་སྐྱོབས་པ་ཐམས་ཅད་ཀྱི།
dak gi déring kyop pa tamché kyi

སྤྱན་སྔར་འགྲོ་བ་བདེ་གཤེགས་ཉིད་དང་ནི།
chen ngar drowa désheknyi dang ni

བར་དུ་བདེ་ལ་མགྲོན་དུ་བོས་ཟིན་གྱིས།
bardu dé la grön du bözin gyi

ལྷ་དང་ལྷ་མིན་ལ་སོགས་དགའ་བར་གྱིས།
lha dang lhamin la so gawar gyi

> And so, today, within the sight of all protectors,
> I summon beings, calling them to Buddhahood.
> And, till that state is reached, to every earthly joy!
> May gods and demigods and all the rest rejoice![50]

This completes the formal or initial practice. The merit we have accumulated is such that we are certain that we will reach the state of enlightenment, in one way or another, no matter our current destination.

The reason to say so is the following: at one time, Buddha Shakyamuni was teaching *The Heart Sutra*[51] at Vultures' Peak. A few hundred ordained monks who were highly experienced and realized were present. They heard the Buddha teaching *The Heart Sutra* and saying:

> Likewise, there is no suffering, no origination [of suffering], no cessation [of suffering] and no path [to the cessation of suffering]. No wisdom, no attainment [of wisdom] and

---

50 *Op. cit.*, p.86, stanza 34.

51 For a translation of the sutra, see *The Gate of Two Merits*, p.161.

non-attainment [of wisdom].[52]

They were suddenly all put off. The master of the group got up and said, "Venerable Sangha, let's go somewhere else," and they left the teaching.

Later on, the close attendance gathered around the Buddha, acknowledged it, and asked the Buddha,

"Are there any negative consequences for these individuals who have left the teaching?"

"Yes, there are."

"Does it mean that anything they have done so far is meaningless?"

"It is not meaningless at all because they accumulated something very precious: the Buddhadharma. Although they may have temporarily been put off—they didn't have the stomach to digest that sacred part of the teaching—nevertheless, in time they will once again come across most profound circumstances, and they will find their way and eventually attain enlightenment."

Practicing the Buddhadharma has great merit, but sometimes our expectations can ruin it. Since we are living in an ever-changing world, any kind of tragedy or obstacle can occur at any moment. Therefore, overexpectations could ruin it, make one lose inspiration, and shake our devotion in the practice of compassion. Therefore, we must realize from here onward that things may change. Nevertheless, the merit will go on unless we have given up on the practice of compassion. We don't need to be surprised if obstacles occur—if we should fall ill or come to the end of this temporary existence. So long as the attitude is not lost, then another favorable condition, or even a more favora-

---

52 *Op. cit*. p.164 for the Tibetan source as well.

ble one, will appear. One will go from strength to strength.

I am not the one to say it; all the previous buddhas and bodhisattvas did over and over again. This is why I have strong confidence in this.

A Specific Meditative Practice: The Preliminary Practice

The Root of All Practices

Buddhadharma has benefitted many generations—in the East, for example. Over and around the Himalayas, Buddhism has given a sense of healthy identity. Even though that is not the aim of Buddhism, it brought contentment and clarity to watch what everything is about. Therefore, it is good to remind ourselves of that and not to waste our favorable external conditions. From different angles, we are at the peak of existence. There is nothing to complain about. In terms of the inner development—particularly for Buddhadharma practitioners—we should recognize that the contentment, the peace, or in other words happiness, has really stemmed from having a very strong devotion to the Buddha's teaching.

The preliminary practice, *ngöndro*[53] in Tibetan, means the practice that comes before and that is behind all practices. Within and around the Himalaya region, this practice is very deeply rooted and common. It is a daily practice that people do at home, in retreat centers, in institutes for higher education, and in monastic and other forms of communities. It has benefitted countless beings.

In short, one could say that it is like the gateway to the practice of Vajrayana that is quite popular by now. One should not understand gateway as if the Vajrayana vehicle is the next step. It is just another labelling. In the end, it is none other than the practice of compassion and wisdom.

It very simply begins with the practice of refuge and the practice of generating loving kindness and compassion toward sentient beings. It is therefore the practice of a bodhisattva. I suppose that in order to give the practitioner a sense of enthusiasm and inspiration, it has a connotation of something sacred, rare, and precious. For this reason, there are various terminologies to describe different forms of practices, but these are just terms—a means to bring inspiration. Thus, it is very important to realize that and clear our mind from the phobia that one is better than the other.

After having generated bodhichitta, we may wonder what the next step is and what we can do or practice. The foundation or preliminary practice is an option then. Indeed, it is not only a first step, but, more than that, it is the basis for all bodhisattva practices.

Therefore, one must never disregard this practice—thinking that it is just for beginners and not for advanced

---

53   སྔོན་འགྲོ

practitioners. In fact, many great bodhisattva practitioners—one should maybe call them advanced practitioners—practiced the ngöndro during all their lives because
they understood that everything we need in our daily lives
in terms of formal method or key practice is included in
this one.

Seeing Things as They Are

Having mentioned that it is a gateway to the practice of
Vajrayana, a few clarifications are needed. First of all, to
summarize, the practice of the Vajrayana is known as the
practice of pure view. This could also be misinterpreted in
many ways. *Pure view* means clear view. It is a practical
approach. It can be simplified by saying that it is basically
the same thing as the bodhisattva attitude or the coura-
geous attitude.

The attitude of a Vajrayana practitioner is based on bodhichitta. The individual views all experiences—whether
mundane or beyond mundane—as not just mere accidents
occurring due to chance or fluke. The practitioner's attitude is that he or she is not limiting him or herself to one
particular perspective of his or her experience of reality,
thinking that suddenly there was a Big Bang and things
came out of it, out of nowhere, and much later, due to human civilization, we are now trying to make sense of all
this. The method provides a perspective to the practitioner
that his or her experience of reality is an extremely extraordinary one, not an ordinary one, meaning that it is
beneficial and meaningful for oneself and for others. Pure
or extraordinary view is not about saying that everything
disappears and that the confused experiences stop right
away. Rather, because of this attitude, every karmic experience and every disturbing emotion that arises starts to
make sense and be meaningful.

57

For example, when experiencing various forms of misfortune and obstacles—material; immaterial; intellectual poverty; physical illness; the loss of someone or something; loss in terms of investment; it could be anything—this extraordinary attitude provides the practitioner with a kind of courage and enthusiasm to recognize that this experience is not completely overwhelming his or her consciousness. It is natural that a jolt or a surprise happens at first, but one is not overwhelmed nor overburdened and completely obscured by it. In fact, one is thus able to recognize that it is the most direct form of teaching of the very state of conditioned existence. No words nor explanations are required.

It is very healthy—refreshing in a way—that one becomes able to observe and recognize each misfortune in this light. This applies to any experience, in fact. If the mind has been influenced by a narrow point of view for a certain period of time—for example the theory that a sense of loss exists—then one is used to thinking that a certain experience is defined as a loss, a misfortune, or an obstacle. The Buddhist practitioner is not being brainwashed or hallucinating. Rather, he acquires a broader perspective and, as a result, instead of seeing something as a misfortune, one is able to recognize that this is not all that. This recognition is a direct information of the experience itself indicating that everything is change; everything is impermanent and there is nothing to hang on to.

The understanding or recognition that everything is impermanent is in general fundamental to a Buddhist. It is seen as a very healthy approach. Our common perspective is that we need to feel that there is something to hang on to. It gives us a sense of stability, that we can look forward to tomorrow, that it might be better than today or that the next moment might be better than this one. It can also be the other way around: that we can hang on to our past, because at least there is a good memory there that we have.

That mode of thinking has its own uplifting quality. Nevertheless, with that way of viewing the world, the mind narrows things down and suddenly leads to a narrow perspective. As a result, it gives birth to afflictive disturbing emotions, either right there or in time. This is part of the karmic process. There are different types of karmic outcomes. Some occur right away and some later on in time. For example, that mode of thinking can give birth to a desire to hang on to the future or to the past. By doing so, karma is also simultaneously, equally generated by trying to preserve this experience or memory in the next moment. As a result, one deploys various forms of means either physically, verbally, or mentally. The means itself are neutral, but because of that mode or narrow attitude, suddenly the means are utilized in such a way that it will automatically generate more agitation and confusion.

From the Buddhist perspective, this is called a common attitude or perspective of reality.

The practitioner's attitude, or the extraordinary perspective, is to view things as they are, without having changed or altered the sight, the object, and the viewing element. One is viewing the experience as it is.

That attitude is also very sensible. If one is not used to it, there will be a slight discomfort. For example, if we have not done any physical exercise for a while and we start again, initially we will experience a sense of cramp. It is the same. Therefore, when one experiences immediate discomfort, one is not put off. One realizes that it is only natural. For example, if there is birth—of anything—then there is likewise death. Therefore, one is not overwhelmed by that realization. In a way, it is having a practical approach to stomach or realize that conditioned existence—the conceptual world—is like that.

That attitude alone gives everything that the practitioner needs to move forward. In the same way, it gives the ability to share the same information with others. Then, as one gets more and more comfortable with or used to that attitude, every experience is not over the top praised or criticized and every experience becomes meaningful and helpful.

Our common way of viewing things and educating and maturing oneself is based on focusing only on what is pleasant and favorable—not out of a negative intent, but out of good and kind intent. The discomforting or unfavorable experiences are somehow left more and more unexplored or unrecognized.

The intent is great; starting from one's own parents, our first teachers in life. Be they biological or not, they try to educate the young ones out of very genuine kindness and compassion in many cases. In order to protect, to guide, and to ensure that each of us will grow up in a peaceful environment—out of love—they try to shield us from all the natural part of life: the misfortunes, the hindrances, the obstacles, and the confusions. There is a practical benefit to it. In the process of growing up, we do need that protection and care. However, gradually what we require is also to have a little more insight as to what life is all about.

The teachers themselves—be they parents or other forms

of teachers—have no way of really knowing what the right way is, when the right time to actually provide the complete experience of life is. They also learned in the same way from their own parents. That is how it goes, all the way back, and there is no real beginning at all.

A bodhisattva is able to recognize that fact. Therefore, during the initial period as a beginner, he or she focuses more on those fundamental and most crucial points that need to be covered first—rather than learning or studying, for example, about the constellations or the next scientific or medical discovery or the next great invention. A practitioner takes time, spends all of his or her energy, to recognize—not really the fundamental drawbacks—but where it gets blurry or confusing in terms of how to *really* care. The potential and quality of caring are present, but a practitioner focuses on how to care in a way that is not demanding or holding oneself or others back.

In some ways, we could think that these formal practices do not really touch our everyday life and that there is no real connection. But actually, the benefit of formal practice is that it actually takes care of the foundation of our attitude, although it may not seem direct enough to our daily experience and how to deal with it.

A Means for Gathering Beneficial Conditions

Step by step, one progresses through the practice of accumulating merit and wisdom, which in short could be summarized as the preliminary practice. This practice is a way to accumulate merit to generate the most favorable conditions. We are trying to liberate ourselves from conditioned existence. In this case, *merit for favorable conditions* may sound contradictory, but the truth lies in realizing what this factor called condition can do. It can in fact be very positive. Therefore, the preliminary practice can be described as acquiring merit, or favorable conditions.

It could be equally contradictory and confusing to hear that the path to enlightenment is about freeing oneself from karma and afflictive disturbing emotions, whereas in this precise case we try to accumulate good, meritorious, virtuous, or positive karma.

The bodhisattva's approach is that each factor or phenomenon is recognized as a neutral or undefined tool. Once there is a direct recognition that karma can work either way—both in a harmful as well as a positive way—one will never, ever intentionally use the tool in a harmful way unless one loses sanity due a great illnesses or mental breakdown. On the contrary, one will make use of karma in the most helpful way.

Therefore, bodhisattvas and buddhas would never criticize any form of technology (conceptual or physical technology of any era) for example. They don't disregard anything, because they understand that it is just a tool. They recognize that medicine, science, religion, politics, economy, etc., can all be turned into something beneficial.

Therefore, one recognizes that the condition we have—human existence and everything that goes with it—is the result of merit. Not just any merit; it comes from having generated different forms of compassion and performing virtuous deeds.

When a deed is performed out of genuine compassion—although it may be limited to a certain extent—the positive result is always inevitable and flawless. It will bear its fruit.

Therefore, at the very beginning of this practice, one focuses on the four thoughts that turn the mind away from samsara[54]: the difficulty of obtaining a well-endowed human existence, the impermanence of life, the infallibility of actions, causes and effects, and the flaws of cyclic existence.

Reflecting on these four thoughts is a way to assist us—in a very formal way—in recognizing that the condition we have now is not the result of an accident or a mere fluke; it came out of merit and kindness.

From there onward, one is formally training oneself to view what could happen if this favorable condition—this merit or karma—is misused: one could meet with very unfavorable circumstances. Then, focusing on the practice of impermanence of life—particularly the fragility of life—is actually a very optimistic and positive approach.

Next, comes the thought on the faults of samsara.

The result of causality—or literally action, cause, and effect—is flawless. Whatever physical or mental action is taken, then the equal, just result will take place. Each of those actions gives a result; it automatically shows that there is an end somehow. When an action—karma—is undertaken, it has a beginning, a middle, and an end. When it reaches a certain stage (the middle), it is most favorable for utilization for whatever one wishes to accomplish. Countless examples in the sutras prove this. One example I can think of is baking bread. Sometimes when I bake bread, the whole process of mixing the ingredients reaches a point where the dough proves most favorable. At that time, I can utilize it to make anything: a pizza, a loaf of bread, or anything else.

---

54 These four reflections are situated at the very begining of the preliminary practice texts, either the one compiled by the 9th Karmapa, Wangchuk Dorje, or that authored by the 14th Shamarpa, Mipham Chökyi Lodrö (p.1b to 2b).

In the same way, bodhisattvas recognize that each of these conditions has its own advantages. Therefore, we can accumulate merit for three eons or for as long as one wishes, but at a certain point it reaches a certain stage when it is most favorable. It is so favorable that it could be transformed into anything. For example, if one reads the life story of the prince Siddhartha, one sees that he obtained the result of having reached that most potent peak. He could have used it in different ways. That is why the astrologists said to his father at the time of his birth that he could turn into a universal monarch or equally become a buddha[55].

In the same way, by gathering merit and wisdom, we will accumulate the most favorable of conditions. The practice of wisdom supports or complements the accumulation of merit in providing skillful means.

You may be familiar with the way the great *arya* Asanga[56] attained realization. He is one of the greatest bodhisattvas who brought forth the Mahayana tradition of Buddhism. The story is, in short, the following: he entered into retreat for twelve years with the aim of realizing the state of Buddha Maitreya. Every three years, he would pause his retreat and search for signs of realization.

The first time he saw a woman fashioning needles out of an iron pole by using a handkerchief. When he saw that, he asked,

"What are you doing?"

"I am fashioning needles by rubbing the cloth on top of the iron pole," the woman answered.

---

55   See Thich Nhat Hanh, p.44.

56   4th century C.E. founding father of the Cittamatra school of thought.

From an ordinary point of view it did not make sense, but he probably took it as a hint and entered into retreat for another three years. He came out in search of signs and met a person using the tip of a feather to rub the top of a mountain. Asanga asked,

"What are you doing?"

"I am trying to dig a hole through the mountain by using this piece of feather."

Asanga was again confused and went back into retreat. For almost twelve years, he searched for signs, but he could never find any proof. After those twelve years, he came out and searched once more for a sign. He was most probably distraught, and he did not feel as if he had realized anything. On his way out of retreat, he found a female dog half eaten by maggots. The dog was left alone in the most terrible state. The maggots could have ended up eating totally the dog. At the same time, he understood that if he tried to use any tool, even his bare hands, to remove the maggots, it could also kill the maggots. Right then, all his searching and yearning for a sign disappeared and all he could experience was an immense sense of care.

The only thing he could think of was trying to remove the maggots from the dog by using his tongue. He thus approached the dog and was about to start licking the maggots away. The habitual pattern or the instinct kicked in as to the notions of pure, impure, pleasant, unpleasant—the worldly *dharmas* as we call them. Yet the compassion was compelling him to continue with the removal of the maggots, and so he closed his eyes and started to lick. As he lowered himself closer and closer to the dog, he could not touch the skin. He had to bend further down and finally his tongue touched the earth. He was surprised and thought he had missed the dog. When he opened his eyes, the dog was no more. Instead, I guess, all he must have seen was a pair of feet! Immediately, he looked up to see who it was, and there was Buddha Maitreya.

Buddha Maitreya must have asked him what he was doing, and Asanga then cried out loud and started to complain, "I have toiled for twelve long years to realize your state. Where were you all this while? Why didn't you show up?"

Buddha Maitreya listened and said, "Actually, I was right there with you—from the first day of your retreat." If I use my imagination, I think he must have said that he was even there before Asanga was born!

"Why did I not see you then? Why now?"

"It is because all this while your compassion and wisdom were not synchronized," to translate it in modern terms, "so as a result, most of the time you were handicapped by using either one of them and never realizing that they are the same. All that time, you lacked compassion. However, this time, when you saw that dog covered with maggots and in pain, you have expressed genuine compassion. It suddenly opened you up, opened your eyes and senses; therefore, now you see me."

The rest is history.[57] The reason why I was thinking about this particular story is that the practitioner of preliminary practice needs to accumulate both merit and wisdom. Wisdom doesn't only mean being intelligent and smart but wise to the point that there is no more differentiation between wisdom and compassion. When Asanga was trying to save both the dog as well as the maggots, he was not

---

57 For a complete version of this story see Butön Rinchen Drup, p.236-241.

trying to be intelligent or smart. Instead, he was driven—overwhelmed—by compassion to try his best to save both. In the same way, when we try to accumulate merit, it has to be in combination. Both merit and wisdom have to be accumulated. The idea is not to gather merit because someone said so, forced you, or said it is good to do so. Accumulating merit comes genuinely from oneself, from the depth of one's heart, out of compassion—and that is wisdom.

Therefore, we need to understand that it is not just another exotic ritual using various objects, brocades, thrones, colorful visualizations and chanting. If that were the case, one would be wasting perfectly good minutes and hours doing nonsense repetitions. However, what one is really doing is using a formal method to understand the importance of realizing the potential of those tools. For example, seeing karma as it is is the most powerful tool of all! Handled with care—that is with loving kindness and wisdom—it can give birth to extraordinary things like Buddhahood.

An Outline of the Four Extraordinary Preliminary Practices

The very first part and the basis of the preliminary practice is taking refuge in the Buddha, Dharma, and Sangha and generating bodhichitta. This is the basis for developing oneself as a bodhisattva, which directly translates into helping oneself to have a very stable ground in order to help others.

The basis for the preliminary practice is none other than having a form of individual liberation vow or pratimoksha vow and, on top of that, the bodhisattva commitment—

that is the bodhisattva attitude. Endowed with both commitments, we are more or less ready to practice the preliminaries. The pratimoksha vow could be any level of individual liberation vow. It is a type of conduct that fits our livelihood, our way of thinking, and the way we behave on a daily basis. The very practice of seeking refuge in the Buddha, Dharma, and Sangha is the most basic and fundamental pratimoksha vow.

Usually, the intent of the pratimoksha vows or conduct is to automatically help one be less busy with accumulating harmful actions, harmful speech, and harmful thoughts. The vows are linked to the behavior of body, speech, and mind. For example, we have a certain set of customs and etiquette that are considered civilized—gentlemanly or lady-like. In the same way the pratimoksha conduct is a type of ethic in relation to physical behavior and mindset that is very complementary to seeking clarity and renunciation of samsara.

The bodhisattva vow focuses much more on attitude. To begin practicing that enlightened attitude, the first thing is the motivation or aspiration. We call it *möpa*[58] in Tibetan. The bodhisattva type or seed can be present right away or require some time. Seeking happiness is already the greatest foundation according to the traditional explanation. On top of that, being naturally moved by a tragedy or an object of compassion or respect is the basis for developing the bodhisattva attitude. Whether the seed, characteristic, or potential is there may differ according to the circumstances and the individuals, but when it is there, it really depends on the individual for it to fully blossom. Therefore, one of the first things one practices is that aspiration.

58 མོས་པ། *adhimukti* in Sanskrit.

Focusing on the quality of the various levels of realization and of Buddhahood brings constant inspiration although one may not have a direct realization of it.

The traditional example explains that the wise captain of a ship continuously described the final destination of the journey so that it brought inspiration to the crew. Although the passengers or the crew may not have actually ever seen the destination before, the captain's description helps them not to be overwhelmed or daunted by the journey when they think about it.

In the same way, on a practical level, we only have a concept of what the real practice of generosity is through the description of prayers such as the *Samantabhadra Aspiration Prayer*:

Atop one particle, there are as many realms as atoms;

In each pure realm, more Buddhas than can be imagined
Reside amidst bodhisattvas, their spiritual heirs.
May I see them and emulate their enlightened activity.

Likewise, in absolutely every direction,
Within the space on the tip of one hair,

There are oceans of Buddhas of past, present, and future,
Oceans of pure realms and oceans of eons.

May I fully take part in this enlightened activity.[59]

---

59 *Op. cit.* note 30. Shamar Rinpoche, p.37-38. ཪྡུལ་གཅིག་སྟེང་ན་ཪྡུལ་སྙེད་ཞིང་རྣམས་ཏེ། ཞིང་དེར་བསམ་གྱིས་མི་ཁྱབ་སངས་རྒྱས་རྣམས། སངས་རྒྱས་སྲས་ཀྱི་དབུས་ན་བཞུགས་པ་ལ། བྱང་ཆུབ་སྤྱོད་པ་སྤྱོད་ཅིང་བལྟ། དེ་ལྟར་མ་ལུས་ཐམས་ཅད་ཕྱོགས་སུ་ཡང་། སྐྲ་ཙམ་ཁྱོན་ལ་དུས་གསུམ་ཚད་སྙེད་ཀྱི། སངས་རྒྱས་རྒྱ་མཚོ་ཞིང་རྣམས་རྒྱ་མཚོ་དང་། བསྐལ་པ་རྒྱ་མཚོར་སྤྱོད་ཅིང་རབ་ཏུ་འཇུག

We do not have a direct experience of the manifestation of those countless universes and oceans of pure lands like an advanced or realized bodhisattva, but we can at least relate to it conceptually and aspire for it accordingly.

The ground that we share and can relate to is the ground of aspiration, known in Tibetan as *möpa chöpé sa*[60]. This means that afflictive disturbing emotions may fly here and there like firecrackers, and various forms of pleasant and unpleasant karmas may likewise appear, which may not be that inspiring at times, but nevertheless we have an opportunity like never before: we can have the time, the energy, and the means to aspire. If there is just a hint of praise, we might get carried away. Likewise, if there is a hint of criticism, we can also get carried away. We don't have to feel uncomfortable about that because we are beginners, and we can accept that fact. Nevertheless, we can continue to aspire for development. Sometimes, discovering our beginner state can bog us down in a way. It is good to acknowledge it and continue to aspire.

Aspiration is not baseless, meaningless, resultless, or merely a satisfactory theory that brings a sense of temporary relief. A genuine aspiration for seeking both liberation and enlightenment is such that it is both promised and guaranteed by buddhas and bodhisattvas that even an instant of such aspiration can be compared to filling all the universe, and still that would not be big enough if one tries to compare or measure its scope in a physical way.

What we are aspiring to is a state of complete awareness—clarity—where all the obscurations are dissolved,

60 མོས་པས་སྤྱོད་པའི་ས། *adhimukticharya bhumi in* Sanskrit. It refers to the way the path is practiced based on aspirations on the paths of accumulation and junction where emptiness is not directly actualized.

all afflictive disturbing emotions are completely understood, and so is the potential of karma.

Based on the two vows, those of individual liberation and
of bodhisattvas, we can proceed with taking up the Vajrayana vow. As explained earlier, Vajrayana is the perspective of pure view. What is a state where the quality of
the mind is fully blossomed? How and what could it manifest? This is the purpose of focusing on the quality of the
teacher.

The quality of the teacher could be a most inspiring subject as well as a touchy one. The form we begin with is the
object of refuge. A beginner needs something tangible. In
this case, it could be the concept of a teacher or the very
practice of devotion itself. It is something one cannot do
away with in order to progress on the bodhisattva path.

This is why, from the first preliminary practice—the refuge practice—onward, we meditate on the teacher. Indeed, we visualize the refuge tree and at its center—according to the lineage of the practice—we meditate the
wisdom aspect that is known as Vajradhara[61] in Sanskrit,
inseparable from the teacher. We don't need to be confused about the difference between the usual visualization
of Buddha Shakyamuni and Vajradhara—in this case it is
the same. The form of Buddha Shakyamuni is known as

---

61 *dorjé chang* རྡོ་རྗེ་འཆང་ in Tibetan.

the highest form of the *nirmanakaya*[62], which is one of the two manifestations of buddha activity, and Vajradhara is known as the *sambhogakaya* form. So Vajradhara is the Buddha.

For the practitioner to have a sense of direction, one understands that Vajradhara represents the qualities of the guide or the teacher. There are various ways to describe what and who this teacher is. In short, focusing on Vajradhara is like focusing on what really stays with us when we think of an object of respect. For example, when we think of our parents, it is not the physical form of one's father or mother, not exactly the voice of that person, nor his or her habitual patterns, but the caring aspect that automatically commands respect.

The moment we think of their kindness, something genuine immediately comes. We don't have to force ourselves to think of it or to behave in a certain way. We may wonder where it is coming from. From the brain? From our thumping heart? From our internal organs? There is no answer, yet it is there. That is that. It is our tangible form of the object of refuge, of respect, of devotion.

That is why we meditate Vajradhara; the form to reach the higher grounds of a bodhisattva. When there are fewer and fewer obscurations until no more afflictive emotions could cause us to return to samsara, then the teacher or the experience comes across to us in the form of Vajradhara.

---

62 Enlightenment is expressed in two forms or bodies: the *dharmakaya* (*chöku* ཆོས་སྐུ། in Tibetan) and the *rupakayas* (*zuk kyi ku* གཟུགས་ཀྱི་སྐུ། in Tibetan). The dharmakaya is the realization of the true nature of all phenomena. It is not a material body. The *rupakyas* are the manifested enlightened forms performing the benefit of sentient beings out of pure compassion: the *nirmanakaya* (སྤྲུལ་སྐུ། in Tibetan) and the *sambhogakaya* (*longchö dzokpé ku* ལོངས་སྤྱོད་རྫོགས་པའི་སྐུ། in Tibetan). The *nirmanakaya* or emanation body is the physical body of a Buddha subject to birth, age, sickness, and death like any sentient being. He can be perceived and interacted with by any ordinary sentient being. The *sambhogakaya*, or body of complete qualities, is a subtle body only perceived by beings of high realization.

Under the Bodhi Tree, when Buddha was about to reach the enlightened state, Mara[63] shot arrows at him. Yet, without having to put up a shield to protect himself or use his miracle powers to do something about it, the arrows just became falling flowers.

The refuge in the format of the preliminary practice enables the practitioner to have an inspiring object, and due to that his or her inspiration never shakes. Thus, the merit and wisdom continuously accumulate.

Everyone is potentially an object of respect. However—even in a non-spiritual context—if we try to focus on or develop respect toward someone who does not have the habit or characteristic of being a caring person, his or her behavior will not really move us. For example, thinking of a stranger does not automatically command respect, whereas thinking of someone who cares for us does so without forcing anything. Therefore, to begin, we use the teacher figure to help us develop gratitude and respect. It is not really about pleasing the teacher, but it is a very skillful means to use that object so that we can let go of the ego. Respect and devotion are a very nice way to say giving up ego.

It does not mean that we just drop the ego altogether right there without proper understanding. Letting go of ego means letting go of misusing this phenomenon. It has its positive qualities such as identifying or being able to differentiate and communicate but more than that is un-

---

63 Mara personifies what can turn the practitioner away from the path to liberation, be it tendencies or afflictive obscuring states. In the sutra, Mara is the one who tried to prevent the Buddha from actualizing enlightenment the night before his enlightenment. One of his schemes was to let his horde throw a rain of arrows at him. For the biography of the Buddha and more details on Mara, see the *Lalitavistara Sutra*, vol.2, p.456.

necessary and simply not needed.

We could also think of any sentient being, which could potentially become—given the choice, the circumstances and the time—a buddha and thus an object of respect. Nevertheless, according to the auspicious connections we call *tendrel*[64], from where one stands the object of respect that can exactly contribute to letting go of ego—to developing devotion—is the teacher: someone who is advanced, experienced, and can lead the way. Therefore, that is our focus.

A practitioner endowed with favorable circumstances[65] who is beginning the preliminary practice should be able to use his or her clear mind to recognize whether a teacher has a bodhisattva quality—the genuinely caring and knowledgeable quality—and is someone who practices what he or she is teaching.

If those characteristics are not present in the individual, then one should also have the clarity or the common sense to recognize their absence. A very healthy approach suggests that it is important to give oneself the right amount of time to reflect on and study this guide. Traditionally, it is said that a period of three years is the right time. However, I think it could mean that one should give oneself the right amount of time or space, so that one is not accepting a guide when one may be very emotional or troubled by tragedies, for example, but rather when one's mind is quite clear and calm.

---

64 རྟེན་འབྲེལ། *nidana* in Sanskrit.

65 Favorable circumstances refer here to the first of the four thoughts that turn the mind away from samsara: the precious human existence, the first part of the preliminary practice known as the common preliminaries. A human existence is enjoying favorable circumstances when freed from the eight unfavorable conditions and endowed with the ten richnesses. For the details, see Gampopa and Jamgön Kongtrul Lodrö Tayé.

In general, every decision made when one is intoxicated or emotional is always regrettable. It is the same when it comes to spirituality; decisions also have to be made when one is quite clear.

There is no binding as such. Each of us may find our guide or teacher in our own way. To me, both the teacher and the student have to be a little suspicious—it is not meant in a negative way but in a healthy way. The teacher is responsible for passing on the tools of practice to the student. Therefore, he also needs to study and understand whether the student practitioner is capable, like an undamaged container, because these tools could be misused by the student and harm him or her and others along the way.

When Milarepa[66] finally found his teacher, Marpa Lotsawa[67] did not give him the teachings right away. Marpa kept examining Milarepa for quite a while.

Both sides should be certain prior to any decision. However, once one has made a commitment, then it is equally important to make sure or at least try one's best not to back off or deviate from that path. Therefore, one also needs patience. Life is indeed impermanent, and samsara is very frightening. Nevertheless, one should never rush.

After the taking of refuge and the generating of bodhichitta in the presence of the refuge tree, we offer our body, speech, and mind in the form of the practice of prostrations. It is both a physical and an oral gesture, since one recites the refuge according to the preliminary practice,

---

66 1052–1135 C.E. See his biography and songs of realization: Tsang Nyön Heruka and Chang, Garma [trad.].

67 1012–1097 C.E. Many biographies are available: see Tsang Nyön Heruka and Ducher, Cécile.

which begins by saying:

དཔལ་ལྡན་བླ་མ་དམ་པ་རྣམས་ལ་སྐྱབས་སུ་མཆིའོ།
palden lama dampa nam la kyap su tchi'o.

ཡི་དམ་དཀྱིལ་འཁོར་གྱི་ལྷ་ཚོགས་རྣམས་ལ་སྐྱབས་སུ་མཆིའོ།
yidam kilkor gyi lha tsok nam la kyap su tchi'o.

སངས་རྒྱས་བཅོམ་ལྡན་འདས་རྣམས་ལ་སྐྱབས་སུ་མཆིའོ།
sangyé tchomdendé nam la kyap su tchi'o.

དམ་པའི་ཆོས་རྣམས་ལ་སྐྱབས་སུ་མཆིའོ།
dampé tchö nam la kyap su tchi'o.

འཕགས་པའི་དགེ་འདུན་རྣམས་ལ་སྐྱབས་སུ་མཆིའོ།
pakpé gendün nam la kyap su tchi'o.

དཔའ་བོ་མཁའ་འགྲོ་ཆོས་སྐྱོང་སྲུང་མའི་ཚོགས་ཡེ་ཤེས་ཀྱི་སྤྱན་དང་ལྡན་པ་རྣམས་ལ་སྐྱབས་
སུ་མཆིའོ།[68]
*pawo kandro tchökyong sungmé tsok yéshé kyi tchen dangden-
pa nam la kyap su tchi'o.*

In the glorious and authentic lamas, I take refuge.
In the yidams, the assembly of supreme beings of the manda-
las, I take refuge.
In the buddhas, the bhagavans, I take refuge.
In the authentic teachings, I take refuge.
In the noble Sangha, I take refuge.
In those endowed with the wisdom eye, the dakas, dakinis,
Dharma protectors, and guardians, I take refuge.

---

68   From the 9th Karmapa, Wangchuk Dorje's preliminary practice text.

We thus offer prostrations to the teacher, who is inseparable from the Buddha, the Dharma, and the Sangha, and to the rest of the assembly, like the various forms of bodhisattvas. In using our speech, we also offer praises, but most importantly through the power of our mind, we mentally generate respect.

From there onward follows the practice of Vajrasattva, Dorje Sempa in Tibetan[69], which can be loosely translated as unchanging attitude. It basically means practicing enlightened attitude. Afterward comes the practice of offering in the form of the mandala and then what is known as the practice of the guide or the teacher: the guru yoga, *lamé neldjor* in Tibetan[70].

Every step is a way—a very skillful means—to let go of one's ego, that force that holds us back from caring wisely. The practitioner accumulates 400,000 recitations, or 100,000 of each of this set—taking refuge and pledging to bodhichitta, the recitation of the hundred-syllable mantra of Dorje Sempa, the offering of the mandala or the universe, and the practice of guru yoga. This accumulation can be put in a very practical context by saying that after a certain limit there is a sense of completion. I think the limit that is set in terms of numbers is a way to give us a sense of direction and also to bring inspiration. There is a sense of satisfaction when we have completed something. However, in terms of the actual practice, the real completion can vary. As a sign or proof of completion of the practice, one can ask oneself whether, through the use of the

---

69 རྡོ་རྗེ་སེམས་དཔའ།

70 བླ་མའི་རྣལ་འབྱོར།

skillful means, one's ego is lessening or not. The aim is to be able to completely let go of the ego. As we are able to exhale the ego, so to speak, at the same time, we are able to freely care for and be compassionate toward others.

Often it is the case—most of the time, actually—that the more we practice the worse it gets. We realize our ego is somehow getting worse. Sometimes, that experience can be such that we feel we are not doing something right or that this particular path or practice is not meant for us. Prior to our practice we all have a common sense that there are really strong disturbing emotions. We recognize those on a general basis, but we have not really been intimate with them. Very much like a neighbor, we know there is a building over there inhabited by people. From time to time we perceive some waves, but nothing more than that. When we practice, we somehow get a bit more personal, closer, and that discovery can be quite overwhelming.

As we read the text, it may not be exactly, blankly saying that our ego looks like this and that now we use that precise tool and hold it in our right hand, etc. It is not obvious in that way. What happens is that we have the idea in the back of our head that this practice or medicine is supposed to conquer the ego. This leads to constant over-the-top expectations. "Now that I have completed this, practiced for that many years, studied such and such, done retreats, visited such holy places, spent time with such venerable *sanghas* and teachers and so on, etc." This kind of expectation is always lingering and is sometimes the cause that is ruining our practice.

We should not be alarmed to suddenly discover that

there is probably far more of this ego and these disturbing emotions. We shouldn't feel distraught and bogged down. Actually, with the help of the practice, we become more aware of the setting we are in. It is not just this body or this mind, but it is the whole setting with our surroundings that we are discovering more and more. In a way, we should be delighted about it because for many years or even lives we never really discovered that. So, we should find a way to rejoice that for the first time we are starting to discover something unknown to us.

Therefore, it is not the case that the practice or the skill-ful means has some loose wiring, is not working, or that there is a fault in the practitioner. It is just a real discovery. Now that we discovered something, we are finally able to make correct decisions. This is what I would call coura-geous attitude, which we need to have in order to make the best use of our opportunity.

Every step of the way is crucial, but when we come to the last practice of the guru yoga, we are somehow not com-pletely inexperienced. We are aware of our surroundings and what our destination is. We thus come to realize that the guru yoga is one of the healthiest practices for oneself and that such practice is not at all a way to worship a per-son but rather a means to understand what the individual we called teacher is most enthusiastic about. Let's take an example. If we are interested in the art of sculpting and we see someone who is good at it—depending on our motiva-tion and aspiration—we will be equally interested in him or her. We do not necessarily want to become this sculptor, but we would like to know what this person is interested in.

In short, the teacher—a bodhisattva or a buddha—that is presented in the preliminary practice and is depicted in a human form, is not interested in anything other than genuinely caring. It is very clear that we are not trying to become this person. Realistically, we can never do that. Therefore, one should keep in mind that, toward the end of this practice, it is only a metaphor when it is said that one receives the four initiations and one's consciousness (i.e. the consciousness of the practitioner who upholds his or her commitments) melts with the guru's wisdom and becomes one with it.

It is a visual and conceptual symbol to remind ourselves or realize that, first of all, the teacher is very much like ourselves—as we can see in the Buddha Shakyamuni *Jataka tales*[71] up to the point when he became enlightened after he gave up his princely life as Siddhartha. This gives us a ground to relate to: for now, there is no way for all the obscurations to be cleared. No matter how obscured and conditioned the mind is, it is impossible, and even more than that it is helpless. From that ground, a person can develop and grow. This is the common ground: someone who becomes a buddha, an enlightened being, also began from where we are beginning. Therefore, this understanding gives us a reference we can relate to on a very grounded level. That is the real melting.

Once we have that common ground, then everything is relatable. Most importantly, we can relate to the actual object of interest: the teacher. He or she is equally inspired by the way of the bodhisattvas, which is exactly what they breathe, practice, and teach. Therefore, every step of the

---

71 The *Jataka* tales recount the previous lives' story of Shakyamuni before he became a buddha, thus showing how past deeds condition future rebirths. The canonical text is the *Jatakamala*, compiled in the 4th century C.E. by Āryaśūra. For translations in English from the Sanskrit, see Āryaśūra.

way, there are countless similar—if not same—interests, and we are trying to rejoice in or focus on that part.

The four reliances, *tönpa zhi*[72] in Tibetan, are a very healthy and helpful way to really be able to become inseparable from the teacher.

གང་ཟག་ལ་མི་རྟོན། ཆོས་ལ་རྟོན།
gangzak la mi tön/ tchö la tön

ཚིག་ལ་མི་རྟོན། དོན་ལ་རྟོན།
tsik la mi tön/ dön la tön

དྲང་དོན་ལ་མི་རྟོན། ངེས་དོན་ལ་རྟོན།
drangdön la mi tön/ ngédön la tön

རྣམ་ཤེས་ལ་མི་རྟོན། ཡེ་ཤེས་ལ་རྟོན།
namshé la mi tön/ yéshé la tön

> Rely on the teaching, not on the person;
> Rely on the meaning, not on the words;
> Rely on the definitive meaning, not on the provisional one;
> Rely on innate wisdom, not on partial consciousness.

One does not rely on the person, but on the person's conduct and practice, called *labpa*[73] in Tibetan. What we are practicing is not the person. We might be led to understand that the guru yoga is a way to become the teacher, which is not wrong in a way, but the exact meaning is that we are trying to actualize the teacher's quality.

---

72 རྟོན་པ་བཞི། *catupratisharana* in Sanskrit.

73 བསྒྲུབ་པ། *karaniya* in Sanskrit.

Prior to practicing the preliminary practice—the same applies for other meditative practices—one should receive the explanations and the reading transmission (*lung*[74] in Tibetan) from a qualified teacher. The reading transmission is very practical. We don't really have to understand it. Rather, we make sure that we at least listen. I would say that it works in the same way as a computer. The consciousness registers all of the intercut series of sounds that is being heard. Whether we understand it or not when we hear it, in reality it will never disappear from our minds. Then, when the moment is appropriate—when one has gained a certain degree of clarity of mind—all that we have received since many rebirths will become clear to us. It is like an integrated databank!

The younger brother of Asanga, Vasubandhu[75], had a pigeon on his roof. Every morning prior to his daily schedule of practice and teaching, Vasubandhu would recite various scriptures and sutras, either by reading or by heart. In the early morning, the pigeon was up there, so he heard everything that Vasubandhu was saying. It went on until the end of the pigeon's life. Soon after the pigeon's death, a boy was born in a nearby town. At the moment the boy could speak he said, "I have to go to a specific place and meet with that person named Vasubandhu." Upon his insistence, his parents took him to the master. Vasubandhu was not really certain of the reason for the meeting, but as soon as the boy saw him, he said right away, "From here onwards, I want to remain as your disciple, please look after me!" Vasubandhu asked the boy why he was so

---

74 ཨཱ་ག་མ agama in Sanskrit.

75 4th century C.E. Famous teacher and abbot of Nalanda university in India. He is the author of the *Abhidharmakosha*. See Buton for details on Vasubandhu's life story, p.241-245.

convinced he had to come meet him. The boy answered, "I remember the various scriptures you used to read aloud." And he recited the very scriptures by heart to the letter. However, sometimes there was a gap—certain pages or subjects were missing—but the boy was able to continue. Later on, they both realized that the gaps happened because the pigeon flew off and could not hear that specific part of the scripture!

This story shows that as long as we are able to listen, what we hear will stay in our minds. The teacher thus has to be careful and read the words very clearly and with good punctuation.

May these few words be of great benefit for all.
Let's dedicate the merit that we have generated to all sentient beings.

These words conclude the teaching of Thaye Dorje, His Holiness the 17th Gyalwa Karmapa.

Dedication

In accordance with the wisdom of the victorious Buddhas and what they have seen:

Ultimately, none of us are born with inherent anxiety or hereditary disease,

None of us are doomed to die to an eternity,

None of us are meant to be permanent like statues,

None of us are cut off in the manner of outcasts,

None of us have come from an alien world to this unique rock we call Earth,

None of us are going to the cemeteries for good,

None of us are inseparably one like a mixed paste,

And none of us are other, being fundamentally angelic or demonic.

However, for those of us who relate to our lives in any of these ways, I pray to the Victorious Buddhas and Bodhisattvas to call upon their natural promise of kindness to guide us from this cyclic whirlpool of thoughts.

And I call upon us to open our hearts instead of opening only our five senses.

Please pray through the timeless methods known as the traditional practices of listening, contemplating, and meditating.

Thaye Dorje, His Holiness the 17th Gyalwa Karmapa

Bibliographic Suggestions

Abhayadatta. *Buddha's Lions: The Lives of the Eighty-Four Siddhas.* Berkeley: Dharma Publishing, 1979.

Āryaśūra. *Garland of the Buddha's Past Lives.* New York: NYU Press, 2009, vol.1 & 2.

Aryasura. *The Marvelous Companion, Life Stories of the Buddha.* Berkeley: Dharma Publishing, 1983.

Buton Rinchen Drup. *Butön's History of Buddhism in India and Its Spread to Tibet: A Treasury of Priceless Scripture.* Boston & London: Snow Lion, 2013.

Chandrakirti, Jamgön Mipham. *Introduction to the Middle Way.* Boston: Shambhala Publications, 2004.

Chang, Garma [trad.]. *The Hundred Thousand Songs of Milarepa*. Boston: Shambhala Publications, 1999.

Cleary, Thomas [trad.]. *Gaṇḍavyūhasūtra, Entry into the Realm of Reality in Cleary, The Flower Ornament Scripture: A translation of the Avatamsaka Sutra*. Boston: Shambhala Publications, 1993.

Ducher, Cécile. *Building a Tradition: The Lives of Mar-pa the Translator*. München: Indus Verlag, 2017.

Gampopa. *The Jewel Ornament of Liberation*. New York: Snow Lion Publications, 1998.

Jamgön Kongtrul Lodrö Tayé. *The Torch of Certainty*. Boston & London: Shambhala Publications, 1994.

Karmapa Wangchuk Dorje. *Sgrub brgyud rin po che'i phreng ba ka + rma kaM tshang rtogs pa'i don brgyud las byung ba'i gsung dri ma med pa rnams bkod nas ngag 'don rgyun khyer gyi rim pa 'phags lam bgrod pa'i shing rta (The Carriage Journeying through the Noble Path, Succession of Daily Recitations Composed from the Immaculate Speech Originating in the Ultimate Lineage of Realization: The Karma Kamtsang Lineage; The Precious Garland of the Practice Lineage)*. Biollet: Kundreul Ling.

Lama Jampa Thaye. *Patterns in Emptiness*. La Remuée: Rabsel Éditions, 2018.

Shamar Rinpoche. *The King of Prayers: A Commentary on the Noble King of Prayers of Excellent Conduct.* Lexington: Bird of Paradise, 2015.

————. The Path to Awakening: *How Buddhism's Seven Points of Mind Training Can Lead You to a Life of Enlightenment and Happiness.* Harrison: Delphinium Books, 2014.

————. The Unity of Merit and Wisdom: *The Preliminaries of Mahamudra as Daily Practice.* 1996.

Shantideva. *The Way of the Bodhisattva.* Boston & London: Shambhala, 2008.

The Gate of Two Merits: Prayer Compilation of the Grand Kagyud Monlam. Kalimpong: Shri Diwakar Publications, 2011.

The Lalitavistara Sūtra, The Voice of the Buddha, The Beauty of Compassion. Berkeley: Dharma Publishing, 1983.

Thich Nhat Hanh. *Old Path White Clouds, Walking in the Footsteps of the Buddha.* Berkeley: Parallax Press, 1991.

Tsang Nyön Heruka. The Life of Marpa the Translator: Seeing Accomplishes All. Boston: Shambhala Publications, 1995.

Tsang Nyön Heruka. *The Life of Milarepa.* New York: Penguin Books, 2010.

Index of Sanskrit and Tibetan words

Sanskrit	Tibetan	Phonetic	Translation[76]
adhimukti	མོས་པ།	möpa	aspiration
adhimukticaryā bhūmi	མོས་པས་སྤྱོད་པའི་ས།	möpa chöpé sa	level of conduct based on aspiration
āgama	ལུང་།	lung	ritual reading
arhat	དགྲ་བཅོམ་པ།	drachompa	arhat
āśaya	བསམ་པ།	sampa	to contemplate, to reflect

---

76 The translation of these terms applies to this teaching and can vary according to other contexts.

aṣṭalokadharma	འཇིག་རྟེན་ཆོས་བརྒྱད།	jikten chö gyé	eight worldly preoccupations
Avalokiteśvara	སྤྱན་རས་གཟིགས།	chenrézi	Chenrezig
āvaraṇa	སྒྲིབ་པ།	dripa	obscuration
bhāvanā	སྒོམ་པ།	gompa	meditate
bodhichitta	བྱང་ཆུབ་སེམས།	jangchup sem	enlightened attitude
bodhisattva	བྱང་ཆུབ་སེམས་དཔའ།	jangchup sempa	bodhisattva
Buddha/buddha	སངས་རྒྱས།	sangyé	Buddha/buddha
catuḥpratiśaraṇa	རྟེན་པ་བཞི།	tönpa zhi	four reliances
dāna	སྦྱིན་པ།	jinpa	generosity
Dharma	ཆོས།	chö	Dharma
dharmakāya	ཆོས་སྐུ།	chöku	absolute body
gotra	རིགས།	rik	kind, type, family, category
guruyoga	བླ་མའི་རྣལ་འབྱོར།	lamé neljor	guru yoga
karaṇīyā	བསླབ་པ།	labpa	training in conduct

92

karma	ལས་རྒྱུ་འབྲས།	lé gyümdré	action, cause, and effect
kleśa	ཉོན་མོངས།	nyönmong	disturbing emotions
maṇḍala	དཀྱིལ་འཁོར།	kilkor	mandala
nidāna	རྟེན་འབྲེལ།	tendrel	interdependent connection
nirmāṇakāya	སྤྲུལ་སྐུ།	trülku	emanation body
pāramitā	ཕ་རོལ་ཏུ་ཕྱིན་པ།	paröltu chinpa	perfection
praṇidhāna	སྨོན་ལམ།	mönlam	aspiration prayer
pratimokṣa	སོ་སོར་ཐར་པའི་སྡོམ་པ།	sosor tarpé dompa	vow of individual liberation
rūpakāya	གཟུགས་ཀྱི་སྐུ།	zuk kyi ku	form body
samādhi	ཏིང་ངེ་འཛིན།	ting ngé dzin	meditative absorption
saṃbhogakāya	ལོངས་སྤྱོད་རྫོགས་པའི་སྐུ།	longchö dzokpé ku	body of complete maturity
saṃsāra	འཁོར་བ།	korwa	samsara
saṃvara	སྡོམ་པ།	dompa	vow, commitment

sūtra	མདོ།	do	sutra
Śākyamuni	ཤཱཀྱཐུབ་པ།	shakya tubpa	Shakyamuni
śarana	སྐྱབས་སུ་འགྲོ་བ།	kyap su drowa	to take refuge, to go under protection
śāstra	བསྟན་བཅོས།	tenchö	commentary, exegesis
śrūta	ཐོས་པ།	töpa	to listen
tantra	རྒྱུད།	gyü	tantra, continuity
utsāha	སྤྲོ་བ།	drowa	enthusiasm
vyavahāra	ཐ་སྙད།	tanyé	designation, concept
Vajradhara	རྡོ་རྗེ་འཆང་།	dorjé chang	Dorje Chang
Vajrasattva	རྡོ་རྗེ་སེམས་དཔའ།	dorjé sempa	Dorje Sempa
Vajrayāna	ཐེག་པ་ཆེན་པོ།	dorjé tekpa	Vajrayana

Publishing finished
in March 2020 by Pulsio
Publisher Number : 4010
Legal Deposit : March 2020
Printed in Bulgaria